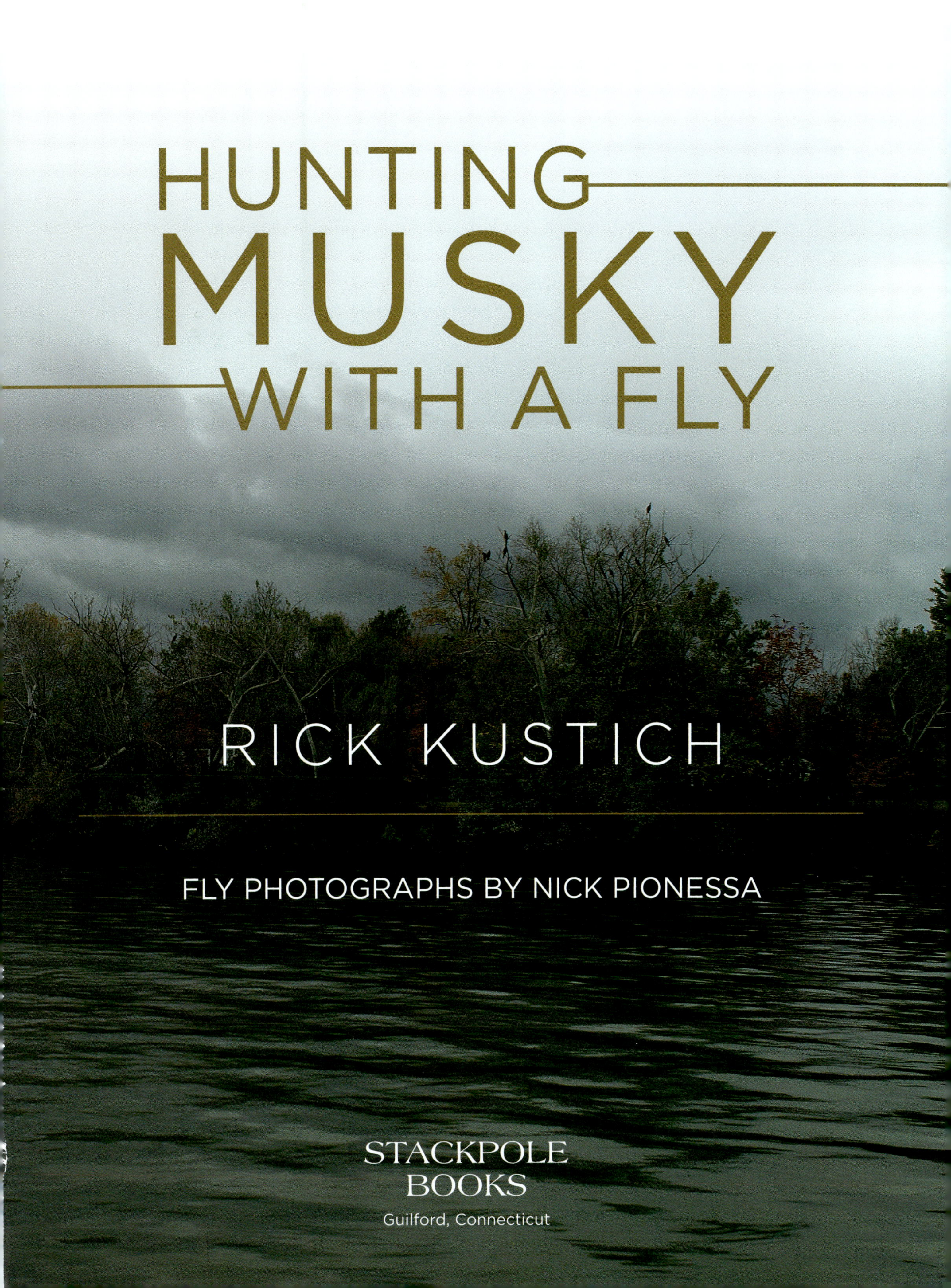

HUNTING MUSKY WITH A FLY

RICK KUSTICH

FLY PHOTOGRAPHS BY NICK PIONESSA

STACKPOLE
BOOKS
Guilford, Connecticut

Published by Stackpole Books

An imprint of Globe Pequot

Distributed by NATIONAL BOOK NETWORK
800-462-6420

All photos by the author unless otherwise noted.
Fly photos and photos on pp. i and iv by Nick Pionessa.

British Library Cataloguing in Publication Information Available

Library of Congress Cataloging-in-Publication Data available

ISBN 978-0-8117-1357-3 (hardcover)
ISBN 978-0-8117-6544-2 (e-book)

Printed in India

CONTENTS

ACKNOWLEDGMENTS

Every book has its supporting cast, but this one had special needs. Due to the limited number of encounters experienced when musky fishing and the wide range of habitat that musky occupy, it would have been nearly impossible to complete a comprehensive guide without the important contributions of top musky fly anglers.

Writing this book has taken me on a long personal journey of discovery. Much was learned directly from years on the water, but a nearly equal share was gained in some way from other anglers. This journey has made me a better angler, and I hope that the lessons learned flow freely through these pages. I am grateful to those who took the time to share their knowledge, their water, or a favorite fly pattern. In the end this is a collaborative effort that represents the views of many musky fly fishers.

A special thank-you goes out to Blane Chocklett and Brad Bohen for hosting me on their waters for multiple outings, taking the time for an interview, and providing their top fly patterns. This special thank-you extends to Eric Grajewski, Bill Sherer, and Chris Willen, whose interviews provide important perspectives.

I extend a special acknowledgment to Steve Wascher for years of companionship and for support in many ways. He was there at the beginning of this process, and one of his signature flies appears in the book. Also, to Joe Goodspeed for some enjoyable days on the water and changing the way I look at musky flies. And certainly to my brother, Jerry, who continues to support all that I do. I have fond memories of our early days chasing musky together—the good ol' days for sure.

The supporting cast includes all those who provided a pattern for the fly chapter, some of the photography found throughout these pages, or their time in some other way. Sincere thanks go to Eli Berant, Nate Carr, Pat Cohen, Ken Collins, Charlie Dickson, Kevin Feenstra, Charlie Gordon, Matt Grajewski, Steve May, Shane Maybush, Jacob Ott, Brian Porter, Mike Schultz, and Mike Small.

I was fortunate to work on this book with editor Jay Nichols. Jay's knowledge of fly fishing added greatly to the finished product, and I am grateful he allowed me to write the book that I had designed in my mind.

A sincere thank-you also goes to my good friend Nick Pionessa. His beautiful photographs are an essential element of the finished product, and his innovative fly patterns also appear in the book. Nick and I have shared many hours on the water together, and he supports my efforts in so many ways with professionalism and dependability.

Last but definitely not least, I want to thank my loving wife, Karen, for her continued support. While I don't think she fully understands my obsessed fly-fishing life, she does so many things to make it all possible.

SWING
THE FLY

INTRODUCTION

My first encounter with a muskellunge, or *Esox masquinongy*, occurred when I was six or seven years old. It wasn't alive, but it was nonetheless captivating. The mount hung in the main meeting area of a fishing club near my home on the upper Niagara River. The club still exists today in its original building and is one of the oldest continuously operated fishing clubs in the country. It was always a treat to be invited to the club by my uncle, and I would stop and stare with fascination at the mount—its mouth agape, displaying a frightening number of sharp teeth. It looked mean. I was amazed that a fish of such character existed in the same river we swam in.

It was a few years before I would actually catch one of the river's muskies. As teenagers growing up on an island, we were fortunate to have access to boats before we were old enough to drive cars. My very first was caught on a hand-tied jig while working deep-water structure for smallmouth. Luckily, the jig's

Good musky management has resulted in healthy populations throughout its range. NICK PIONESSA PHOTO

hook landed in the corner of the musky's mouth and stayed clear of its razor-like teeth. A number of subsequent encounters—some successful and others not so much—fueled my interest.

The first on a fly came around 1990. It was inevitable that my nearly insatiable interest in fly fishing would intersect with the healthy musky population at my doorstep. This step into fly fishing for musky was deeply influenced by a Larry Dahlberg article. In the article Larry described targeting early-season musky in shallow water with a fly using sight-fishing techniques. The article also introduced me to the Dahlberg Diver and reinforced the importance of the double haul. Soon after absorbing this information, my first fly-caught musky was brought to the net.

It wasn't until pursuing musky with a fly that I truly became a musky angler. I began a learning experience that has spanned much of my adult life and most certainly will never be complete, providing me with the motivation to get to the water as much as possible.

To this day I can't pass by a mount or replica of a musky without staring with the same fascination as a wide-eyed young boy. In a day and age where catch-and-release fishing has proven to be so important to the ongoing health of musky fisheries, full skin mounts are certainly passé, representing a testament to the past. But I enjoy hearing or imagining the story behind every musky mount or replica that I see, and draw a connection to that very first visual encounter so many years ago.

Musky management has evolved tremendously in the last 20 years. Despite the difficulty in catching one, musky populations have historically suffered from abusive angling practices. Muskies have a fairly slow growth rate combined with a top-of-the-food-chain status that maintains numbers in line with their biomass. History has shown that excessive pressure on any musky population that involves keeping and killing fish will quickly have a detrimental impact. And the impact isn't just felt by the loss of an individual fish—it also affects future breeding when good genetics are removed from the pool.

Esox masquinongy is also susceptible to habitat degradation. Even though its outward appearance is intimidating and nasty, as a species musky are actually quite sensitive. Changes to delicate spawning areas due to riparian development can have a significant impact on natural reproduction, and musky populations have been lost when human activity eliminated preferred spawning habitat. In some cases habitat can be restored, but in others it seems to be lost forever.

The good news is that professional managers have taken an active role in managing current musky populations. This effort is driven by an interest in preserving or restoring the past along with the desire to provide the opportunity to pursue trophy-size fish in inland waters. Habitat restoration projects have succeeded in improved spawning rates. Even more successful have been population restoration projects where adding planted fish to a lake's or river's natural population has improved overall numbers and increased the metrics for successful spawning.

However, most of the improvement in recreational musky fishing can be attributed to higher size limits and an overall awareness among anglers of catch-and-release. The lower size limits historically found in many areas were not even high enough to allow fish to reach proper spawning age, but that has now changed in most states. Actually, catch-and-release has become the norm on most musky waters. It is an ethic promoted by fishing clubs and even government agencies to increase awareness and maximize the quality of the fishery. Many better options exist for table fare than a musky, and with the beautiful replica mounts available to anglers these days, there is no reason whatsoever to kill a trophy for a skin mount.

I witnessed firsthand what impact active management has on a musky population. In the 1970s the legal limit on the Niagara River was 32 inches. Populations floundered even under limited fishing pressure because fish were not allowed to mature and add to the production potential of the fishery. Over time legal limits were raised steadily to 42 inches, then to 46 inches, and finally to 54 inches, effectively creating a catch-and-release fishery. The local musky club, working with professional managers, was instrumental in making these progressive changes.

For an angler, the Niagara was a musky paradise in the late '80s and throughout the '90s. Populations suffered around 2005, most likely related to a disease that affected the Great Lakes drainage. But numbers are bouncing back nicely, helped once again by the generous kill limits that require almost every fish to be released. This has resulted in an expanding population with a good stratification of year classes.While

The opportunity to catch a trophy musky on a fly has never been better. ERIC GRAJEWSKI PHOTO

stocking programs have had the most profound success in restoring native populations, fishery managers are also using hatcheries for maintenance. Some bodies of water that have lost critical spawning areas rely on annual plantings to retain what once existed. Hatcheries are also instrumental in expanding the musky's presence beyond its historic native range. As someone who appreciates intact habitats, there is something special about wild, native fish of any species. But hatcheries are working to fill in the missing pieces and feed an interest in musky fishing that is, in turn, creating a greater desire in anglers to protect the overall resource.

So what does this all mean? The opportunity to catch a musky in North America is extremely good. In fact, with the advancements in fly-fishing equipment, flies, and available information, the possibilities for taking a musky on a fly have never been greater. The golden age of musky fly fishing is upon us right now.

Hunting Musky with a Fly is not the first word on pursuing *Esox masquinongy* with a fly rod, and it most certainly will not be the last. It is designed to be part of the progression and growth of this element of the sport.

While a good percentage of anglers in North America are fly fishers, musky fly fishers represent the fringe element—explorers and renegades pushing the limits of what fly fishing has historically represented. They are anglers searching for a challenge who appreciate the cunning and ferocity of the ecosystem's top predator. Musky fly anglers are comfortable enough in their own skin and with their fishing abilities that their egos can handle fishless days. It is a growing brotherhood of anglers driven by the excitement of the pursuit and the fascination with a fish that is difficult, if not impossible, to figure out.

The learning curve was slow for me in the early days of my fly-rod musky pursuit. Because little was written on this aspect of fly fishing, my approach was based mainly on techniques that worked for other species and simple trial and error. Proving theories was hindered by the relatively low number of encounters. However, the recent growth in musky fly fishing has led to an explosion of knowledge. And while most musky anglers prefer to keep their prime spots to themselves, the sharing of techniques and flies has rapidly increased the ability of more anglers to enjoy the sport.

Anglers and professionals such as Bill Sherer, Brad Bohen, Blane Chocklett, Eric Grajewski, and Steve Wascher, among others, have pushed musky fly fishing forward with innovative strategies, approaches, and flies. The objective of *Hunting Musky with a Fly* is to excite anglers about pursuing old Mr. Esox with a fly rod while educating readers on the intricacies of this aspect of fly fishing—based on both personal experience and detailed input from the top musky fly anglers in North America.

Fly fishing for musky may not be for everyone because it entails casting big flies on heavy rods for hours with the expectation that one or two fish in the net is a great day. Being serious about the pursuit takes a level of dedication. However, it is a sport that can be enjoyed at various levels. Encountering and catching a musky on a fly is something that every serious fly angler should experience. And the opportunity has never been better.

1 PROFILE OF A PREDATOR

Esox masquinongy has been called the fish of 10,000 casts. This statement speaks volumes about the fish's aloof style and about the dedication of the fanatical angler in its pursuit.

The musky is the largest member of the pike family. "Musky" is short for muskellunge or maskinonge, as it is officially known in Canada, which is a derivative of the Ojibwe word *maashkinoozhe*, meaning "ugly pike."

Joe Goodspeed shows off a beautiful fly-caught musky.

A look into the eye of a predator.

The musky has an elongated body shape similar to a pike, with dorsal, pelvic, and anal fins set well back, providing for quick bursts of speed. It has a flat, wide head with a mouthful of sharp, angled teeth that can put a death grip on its prey. The musky is a true predator. It is capable of viciously attacking unsuspecting prey after lying in wait or silently stalking a potential meal and only making a move when an opportunity is presented.

A musky can live as long as 20 years. While growth rates in some waters can be slow, their longevity combined with an adequate source of food allows a musky to reach a significant size. The size of an average fish in most waters is 30 to 38 inches in length and about 8 to 16 pounds. Where the proper forage base exists, muskies can grow much larger. Thick-bodied fish exceeding 40 inches can be found in most waters where musky exist, and the top fisheries occasionally produce fish that exceed 50 inches. The recognized record for a musky caught on conventional tackle is the much-debated 1949 catch of Louis Spray that occurred near Hayward, Wisconsin, weighing nearly 70 pounds. Over the years the record and actual size of the musky has been questioned and even discredited based on photos of the fish being held by the angler. The photos seem to show a fish that doesn't support a fish of that weight. The actual skin mount of the fish was destroyed in a fire of the tavern owned by Louis Spray. But the record has survived, and this story just adds to lore that surrounds the pursuit of musky.

One could make the argument that every musky caught on a fly is a trophy. There certainly is much truth to this claim, because it can be challenging to land one of any size. But I think a musky of 40 inches or better is quite a feat, and any over that size on a fly is a great accomplishment.

Musky are indigenous to only North America and were originally found in the Great Lakes region and the upper Mississippi drainage. The natural range of the musky is expansive, reaching from New Jersey north into Quebec, westward through Ontario, and ending in the northwest portion of that province. The range moves south, with historic native populations in New York, Pennsylvania, Ohio, Michigan, Wisconsin, and Minnesota. The natural range also reaches into part of Indiana, West Virginia, Virginia, and Kentucky and as far south as Tennessee, North Carolina, and even northern Georgia. The native range consists of spotty distribution. Indigenous musky were mainly confined to certain drainages and specific geographic areas, with most of the indigenous lakes and rivers found in Wisconsin and Ontario.

Plantings of either purebred or hybrid musky have greatly expanded the population of the species. Stocking programs in various states have increased the populations of native waters and introduced the fish to waters that were not historically home to musky. Some of these plantings have resulted in naturally occurring populations, while others continue to be sustained through annual stockings. States that have benefited

Author displays a Great Lakes strain musky.

most from these stocking programs include Indiana, Illinois, Iowa, Maine, Missouri, Nebraska, New Jersey, and both North and South Dakota. Stocking programs have had a significant impact on angling opportunities and are partly responsible for the increase in the popularity of musky fishing. About 45 percent of the lakes and rivers that hold musky today benefit from some level of stocking.

Three recognized subspecies of muskellunge exist within its indigenous area: the Great Lakes strain, the Ohio or Chautauqua, and the tiger or northern musky. The Great Lakes strain originally populated the Great Lakes, its tributaries, and connecting waterways. The Ohio or Chautauqua subspecies is indigenous to the Ohio River valley and populated areas of New York, Pennsylvania, Ohio, and southward. The tiger or northern subspecies was originally found throughout Minnesota, Wisconsin, and southern Ontario.

The three musky subspecies vary in appearance. The Great Lakes strain has a lighter general appearance, with more of a spotted pattern across its body to form oblique rows. The Ohio strain is marked with dark spots or blotches to form indefinite crossbars on the sides. It has more of a green or bronze appearance than the Great Lakes strain, although some are lighter in color. The northern subspecies also has a green or bronze look, with markings that show as faint blotches, bands, or stripes.

Each subspecies has the potential to grow fish over 50 inches. The variations in the subspecies' appearance seem to provide a camouflage advantage in their home waters. The ranges of the various subspecies do not appear to overlap, and despite stocking programs that have expanded the musky's overall range, the indigenous strains have remained remarkably intact.

History

The combination of the musky's potential size and its overall mystique has drawn the attention of anglers for decades. Historical accounts dating back to the

Hatcheries play an important part in musky management.

mid-1800s tell of a musky heyday in parts of Wisconsin, New York, and Ontario. Anecdotal tales of leviathan fish can be readily found in fishing and history books, and often include supporting photographs of anglers hoisting catches of multiple fish. Size and daily kill limits were obviously liberal. It would be a while before the idea of catch-and-release was introduced.

Even though muskies can be difficult to catch at times, it was proven from the late 1800s through the mid-1900s that a fishery could only withstand so much unabated fishing pressure. Popular waters began to show serious declines, and musky populations were reported to be extirpated in certain waters by the turn of the century. This was a trend that continued into the mid-1900s, resulting in multiple populations being either entirely wiped out or below a self-sustaining level. Musky populations seem to be especially susceptible to overharvest because only a limited number of fish exist in each watershed. Also, musky growth rates tend to be relatively slow, so the removal of a mature fish can leave a hole in year-class structure and eliminate the passing of important genetics to future generations.

Overfishing wasn't the only factor that had a significant historical impact on musky populations. Despite the portrayal of the muskellunge as a tough, fierce predator, as a species it is fairly sensitive to disruption of its habitat. Changes in the makeup of critical spawning areas can be devastating to the production of healthy year classes of juveniles. Logging practices, pollution, and land development along lakes and rivers were all factors that had a negative impact on water quality and the sandy or muddy flats required for spawning. Poor logging practices caused excess silt to enter rivers during runoff, covering potential spawning areas and changing the chemical balance of the water. Along popular lakes, shoreline development took its toll. A common negative factor was the construction of break walls to prevent shoreline erosion; these structures dramatically changed the character of important bays and shallow flats used for spawning.

Overfishing and habitat destruction was a one-two punch that led to a significant reduction of musky populations in some rivers and lakes and to their entire elimination in others. Daily size and kill limits were eventually established and tightened throughout the 1900s, and environmental consciousness increased at the same time. This was enough to save many musky fisheries that had not been too badly damaged, but it was too late for many other rivers and lakes. The idea of hatcheries and fish culturing was seen as a solution to the problem of disappearing populations.

The first muskellunge was reportedly cultured at Rice Lake in Ontario in 1876, but the first full management and culture operation occurred on the banks of Chautauqua Lake in New York in 1888 in the vicinity of Greenhurst. A permanent musky hatchery building was then constructed in Bemus Point in 1904 and moved across the lake in 1973, where a state-of-the-art facility produces fingerlings for Chautauqua Lake and other area waters. Throughout the 1900s hatchery operations began at a number of sites within the musky's natural range and figured prominently in defining the current structure of North America's musky population.

Throughout the latter part of the 20th century and into the 21st, musky management took on more of a holistic approach. While hatcheries are still an important management tool in some states, a shift has occurred in management objectives to provide for a quality fishery. Size limits have increased steadily in recent years to allow fish to reach sexual maturity and to improve quality by allowing an undersized fish to be caught more than once. Some of the size limits are state- or province-wide, while others target certain rivers or lakes to provide further restriction.

Released to fight again.

Other main management objectives include rehabilitating damaged habitat and conserving important native stocks. The reintroduction of musky into native watersheds or introduction into new waters through stocking remains a top priority for professional managers. Some of these stocking projects have produced substantial results and significant fisheries, and a few have resulted in impressive occurrences of natural reproduction.

The main factor contributing to the quality of musky fishing today is awareness, and it is possible that opportunities currently rival those of the 1800s. Angler understanding of the importance of catching a fish more than once has led to a high incidence of catch-and-release fishing. This extends beyond fly fishers to gear anglers as well. Live release of mature fish is one of the best management tools for healthy, quality musky populations.

The catch-and-release ethic is being promoted by musky clubs and even some state agencies. With the advancement of photography and replica mounts, there is absolutely no need to keep a fish as a trophy. Most serious musky anglers would agree that a true trophy is one captured in a photo or even just in memory and is released to spread its genes to future generations or to simply allow its story to live on for years.

Behavior

Musky behavior can seem widely complex and at the same time incredibly simple. Musky are driven by the same factors that influence most species: food, propagation, and security. From a security standpoint, mature muskies generally do not fear other fish, and optimum holding areas may have to do more with food and reproduction than with keeping safe. But mature fish certainly have a security-based instinct that is evidenced by the difficulty in fooling a big musky. Understanding these factors and how each relates to your home waters will have a significant impact on success.

For a musky to grow to trophy-size proportions, it must have ready access to a food source. While food may not be the most important positioning factor, it is an essential piece of the puzzle that can cause a musky to stay in one place most of the season or to roam as bait patterns change. From an angling standpoint, it is important to have a basic understanding of a musky's diet in a particular piece of water. And a musky's menu can vary widely from one body of water to the next depending on availability.

A musky's opportunistic approach means that just about anything living is a possible food source, and the menu may include large insects, crayfish, small mammals, and waterfowl. But a high percentage of a musky's diet will be composed of protein-rich fish. Suckers, ciscoes, shiners, bullheads, tullibees, mooneyes, carp, and even exotics such as rudds and gobies will be sought-after food sources when present. A musky's diet can also include juvenile gamefish such as bass and walleye; and despite their spines, musky seem to have a certain fondness for panfish such as perch and crappie.

Understanding the available food in a body of water will assist you not only in fly design, but also in finding high-percentage holding areas. Musky will follow a food source and change their holding areas accordingly. My home river has an abundance of emerald shiners, which are small baitfish commonly referred to as minnows. Because so many other fish use the emerald shiner as a food source, it can have a significant influence on the river's food chain. Areas on the river that contain an abundance of emerald shiners will have the highest concentrations of musky. I have often experienced the full food chain in action, with gulls and terns feeding on the bait from above and bass or other smaller predators attacking from below. When this situation occurs, muskies are usually not too far away. The connection to bait may not be as obvious on some bodies of water, but musky will search out protein and even move from one holding area to another to follow bait migrations.

Seasonal water temperature changes also have a profound impact on musky behavior. Water temperatures below 40 degrees, as typically found in the northern part of the musky's range during the winter months, will dramatically slow their metabolism. While fish will continue to feed, it won't be at the same pace as when the water is warmer. Winter water temperatures in the southern portion of the musky's range will remain above 40 degrees for a longer period of time than in the northern zone.

Understanding the musky forage in the areas that you fish will aid in fly selection.

As water temperatures warm up into the mid to high 40s in late winter and spring, musky behavior will be driven by the urge to spawn. Even in waters that are mainly supported by stocking, fish will typically go through all the motions. Musky will generally be found in shallow water until the temperatures warm into the mid to high 50s. Fish will spawn on sandy or gravel flats, sometimes in areas that are highly visible.

One or more males will swim slowly alongside a female that is readying to deposit her eggs over the bottom as she continues to move across the spawning area. The male or males will then attempt to fertilize the eggs as they are dropped. The males can be aggressive toward the female during this process, pushing or even biting her to encourage the egg-laying process. The fishing season is closed in many jurisdictions during this time, but it is important for anglers to avoid fishing for spawning musky. Even in the most fertile musky waters, spawning success rates are incredibly low. Angling pressure can have a serious negative impact on the health of a musky population.

As spawning concludes, musky will generally remain shallow for a short period of time, slowly increasing health and body weight after the rigors of procreation. During this period musky will stay close to their spawning area along emerging weed beds, but as water temperatures rise into the upper 50s and low 60s, the movement will begin toward summer holds. In smaller lakes this may result in a short movement to their summer range, but in large bodies of water the migration can be significant, adding to the difficulty of locating musky during this transition. Musky will commonly be found in areas that transition from shallow to deeper water and will begin relating to their summer structure and searching out weed beds. In many waters, finding weeds at this time of year will provide a direct link to locating musky because bait will also readily relate to the emergent vegetation.

Water temperatures that reach well into the 70s in the mid to late summer can ramp up a musky's metabolism. Feeding occurs more frequently at this time of year. Fish may stay close to a home range throughout the summer, making adjustments to holding areas as conditions change. Water temperatures dropping into the 60s marks the beginning of the fall transition time. Musky may begin to use edges along open water and be positioned slightly deeper than during the summer. In the fall, with water temperatures dipping into the 50s, musky will commonly leave their summer range as weed beds and other vegetation begin to disappear. Bait will also be transitioning at this time, and musky may follow the migrations of forage fish to maintain a steady source of protein. The weeds that remain into early autumn will attract and temporarily hold transitioning musky.

A post-spawn musky caught in shallow water. NICK PIONESSA PHOTO

As water temperatures drop through the 40s, muskies will generally be found deeper in the column and in rivers may search out the greatest depths. While their metabolism begins to slow, this is the time of year to pack on some body weight by concentrating on a high-fat diet. While a musky may not eat as often in the fall as in the summer, the focus will now be on larger forage. Fly size should be adjusted accordingly. With shorter daylight periods, feeding activity also will be more concentrated, giving the appearance that musky are feeding as often as in the summer. These conditions represent the best opportunity to tangle with a true trophy-size musky on the fly.

When water temperatures drop into the 30s, musky may move away from defined structure into more open areas. In rivers this will generally include deep, slow pools. As metabolism slows, musky still remain active enough to relate to the movements of the forage base. Positioning during the winter will often be affected by the proximity to spring spawning areas. Locating near traditional breeding grounds allows a musky to begin the process when the proper conditions are present without wasting stored energy by traveling.

This annual cycle varies based on geography. Areas in the southern region of the musky's range experience higher water temperatures in the winter months than those in the north. These conditions create a longer growing season and a prolonged fall transition. Good fishing opportunities exist through the late fall and winter months on some southern rivers, as fish will remain active right up to the spawn. Also because of water temperatures, the breeding period shifts on southern rivers, with the spawn occurring in March and April in the South and normally May and June in the North.

Fishing regulations vary widely throughout the musky's range. In some jurisdictions the season remains open all year, while in others angling is restricted during the winter and spawn. Be sure to check the local regulations, as some prohibit targeting fish that are out of season even if catch-and-release is intended.

Water level and clarity can both have an impact on musky behavior. Clear water conditions generally make muskies more cautious with their approach. This increase in cautious behavior can be even more noticeable on rivers when clear conditions are combined

Autumn can be the best time to hunt for trophies. Chris Willen displays a good one. CHRIS WILLEN PHOTO

Green water with some stain creates perfect conditions. NICK PIONESSA PHOTO

with low water. Water that is slightly to moderately stained from rain, wind, or algae blooms seems to give the predator an advantage and can put musky on the hunt. It also is easier to fool a musky on a fly when the water is not ultra clear.

Water-level changes on rivers also directly impact expected musky behavior. As the water level rises, the change in flow displaces baitfish and other sources of food, creating vulnerability of the prey. The displacement of bait and the stain in the water that commonly accompany rising levels creates the perfect combination of factors for a predator to go on the hunt. It is a behavior that can also be observed in brown trout in rivers and streams. However, the river level may reach a point where it is simply too high, forcing all fish into more of a survival and security mode.

Some of the best conditions on a river exist as water levels begin to recede and clear after a high-water event. After a period of inactivity brought on by high, dirty water, clearing conditions once again place musky on the hunt. Bait settles back into its normal holding areas, creating opportunity. A musky can be very aggressive and more likely to grab a fly when it shows interest under these conditions.

Moon Phases

Observations I have made during a lifetime of fishing and hunting have shown that the influence moon phases have on the activity of fish and game is pronounced. From affecting the amount of available light for movement and feeding to varying the intensity of gravitational pull, the change of the moon can cause some behaviors that are nearly predictable. The impact of the moon can be seen in musky behavior and is an important factor when choosing which days to be on the water.

Musky can be caught throughout all moon phases. Some of the top musky fly-fishing guides that I have interviewed do not pay close attention to moon phases, since they will generally be fishing each day anyway.

The moon can have a significant impact on musky behavior. NICK PIONESSA PHOTO

But the moon phase impacts the level of activity that will be encountered and the opportunity to catch a trophy-size fish.

Both extremes of the moon phase tend to bring on increased musky activity. The new moon and full moon, including the days surrounding these points in time, consistently produce some of the best opportunities for a musky to commit to taking your fly. I have experienced many days during the new moon period where the number of muskies encountered well exceeded the average experience for that body of water. The lack of available light at night most likely forces a more concentrated feeding effort during the daytime.

The full moon brings with it a similar increase in activity and seems to have a general impact on overall musky feeding. Muskies will readily feed during the day and night under the full moon, with midday feeding often experienced. The increase in feeding under a full moon may be a result of a general increase in the activity of forage fish predicated by the overall amount of available light. But fishing under a full moon can also be frustrating as the amount of available light allows musky to feed over a wider period reducing your odds of an encounter.

The increase in opportunity to fool a musky during the new moon seems to include the days leading up to the new moon. My records indicate that the last quarter leading up to the new moon is the most productive of the moon's four quarters. The full period also extends past the date of the full moon. The three to five days following the full moon can also provide an increase in musky activity. This full-moon and post-full-moon period can bring some of the biggest fish to a fly and represents one of the best times to fool a true trophy musky.

Within the various moon phases, the daily rise and set of the moon has been shown to have a direct, and significant, correlation to musky activity. After tracking it the past few years and referring to my notes for the years before, the evidence is overwhelming. There is clearly an increase in the number of hookups and

Overcast and rainy—perfect musky conditions. NICK PIONESSA PHOTO

encounters that occur in the hour to 45-minute period before and after a moonset and moonrise. And while most of us get out on our favorite musky water when time permits, I find myself timing my outings to coincide with the moonrise or moonset and trying to be on my best water during the occurrence.

The daily rise and set of the sun also spurs an increase in musky activity. This increase in activity is most likely the result of light conditions that favor the predator. Low light allows a musky to feel comfortable in roaming and hunting, and it can take advantage of food sources that move away from their protective structure during the cover created by the low-light conditions. Some of the best musky feeding activity can be experienced in the one-and-a-half- or two-hour period surrounding a moon or sun rise or set.

Weather patterns can enhance or trump the effect of a favorable moon position. I prefer cloudy conditions to sunshine, especially in clear-water rivers and lakes. Like most predators, bright light can make a musky more wary. The negative effects of sunshine seem to be mitigated in tannic or stained water. Stagnant weather patterns that create extreme high or low barometric pressure readings can put musky in a stale mood, but a change after a period of stable weather can really put fish on the move. An approaching storm front with a changing barometer creates the perfect scenario for musky activity. Combine that with a favorable moon phase, and the possibilities are endless. Even minor fronts that bring in light rains after a prolonged period of sunny weather can generate increased feeding activity, and I have experienced some of my most memorable days under these conditions.

One could argue that the best time to go musky fishing is any time you can. And musky are unpredictable enough that merely having your fly in the water under any condition gives you a chance of hooking a fish. But some of these behavioral factors can be used to your benefit to greatly increase the odds, especially on larger fish. When possible, planning outings or trips around optimum moon phase, temperature, and weather periods can pay big dividends.

Low light periods can be very productive.

Brian Porter displays a hefty late autumn Wisconsin trophy. BRIAN PORTER PHOTO

2 GETTING YOUR HEAD IN THE GAME

A mature musky is the apex predator in any ecosystem where it lives. This standing in the food chain allows the musky to operate with a certain attitude and swagger—basically doing what it wants when it wants. It can be viciously aggressive or passively aloof, and the change from one to the other often occurs instantaneously and without warning. Its unpredictability keeps you constantly on your toes. It is the musky's odd behavior that both captivates and intrigues, creating a magnetic draw in attempting to understand its habits and connect with the fish in its own domain.

You must be prepared on all levels to go the distance. NICK PIONESSA PHOTO

Being at the top of the food pyramid in itself limits the number of musky that will be found in any fishery. Combine this with its preference for larger meals, reducing the number of feeding occurrences per day, and statistically the odds are stacked against the fly angler. The fly needs to be presented in a precise place at a time when the mood is right and an aggressive fish is ready to eat.

Often it takes some convincing to get a musky to commit to the fly. Muskies are known for their behavior of following the retrieve of the fly right to the rod tip. It is exhilarating to witness a large fish swimming inches behind the fly, but it can also be frustrating if the fish swims away without a take. Certain techniques used right at the boat can change your fortune. These close-quarter encounters are the hallmark of musky fishing and keep you coming back time and time again.

Musky fishing is rarely about numbers. While there are days when multiple fish are brought to hand, it is more often about the experience and finding that one fish that remains indelibly etched into memory. Catching a musky by any means can be difficult, but add the factor of fly fishing, and you have accepted freshwater's greatest challenge. It is a challenge that requires at least a minimum commitment but more importantly preparation on all levels. Being properly prepared includes the basics of having the right equipment, rigging, and flies and extends to also being ready both mentally and physically.

Success is often measured in the accomplishments of the day. Encounters of any nature, including hookups and musky sightings, go a long way toward learning new holding areas and maintaining an overall level of excitement. Something can be learned from every encounter, even if it is simply becoming more comfortable and under control when a big musky is within a couple of feet of the rod tip. The number of encounters experienced when fishing your favorite piece of water is an important factor in measuring the day's productivity.

In a sense, you are always working toward the next hookup. Data and information that are gathered during the course of a day may assist in that effort. Other positive reinforcement such as a follow or a hookup on a new fly pattern or a new rigging method can also provide important input for the future. Maintaining detailed notes of your fishing experiences is a way to document accomplishments as well as assess certain trends that develop on the waters you regularly fish.

Every cast should be delivered with confidence and the belief that it could be *the* cast that will hook a musky. Without that level of self-assurance, it is probably time to change your location or fly. But it takes an acquired knack to know when the time has arrived to change course. You should not make decisions out of impatience, but rather with calculated moves based on experience and reasonable expectations for the water being fished. Having a balance of realistic expectations and confident persistence provides the proper approach for success.

Daily expectations on any good musky water include having at least one direct encounter. This is a good baseline objective, and when conditions are right, this target can readily be exceeded where good fish populations exist. Sometimes it takes a number of encounters to actually bring a musky to the net or cradle. One of the keys to successful musky fly fishing is to maintain the right frame of mind throughout the day. This requires a cool focus. Close attention should be paid to every cast and retrieve—finishing each with the belief that a fish is about to take the fly. But it is critical to remain relaxed so that faced with an encounter with a big musky, you can react calmly to the situation with a positive response. It is also critical to maintain this focus even after recent encounters have not worked out as well as possible. Disappointment is a part of fly fishing for musky.

Working through the ups and downs of musky fishing is essential to consistently taste success. Often things do not go as planned, but continuing to cast and fish with a purpose and maintaining the belief that something good could happen on each cast is essential. Periods of unsuccessful outings can wear on your ego and psyche, but working through the tough times is always rewarded in the end.

Finding small victories any place you can is the key to passing through the lows. While these small victories will include tallying up quality encounters, they can also include making improvements in casting, presentation, boat control, fly design, or any other important detail that directly result in a landed musky. Identifying new potential holding water is one of the most positive outcomes of a day on the water.

In musky fishing, your entire season can turn around in one cast. And once things start going in a positive direction, it often continues. Success seems to breed success. Catching a fish leads to a certain relaxed, confident state that in turn leads to more landed fish. That is why it is so important to be able to stay in the game throughout the day.

Musky fishing is about effectively and efficiently covering water. It is a statistical game of consistently placing the fly in the likely right spot. Every good cast and presentation only increases your odds. Making your best cast every time, even when the prospects look bleak, goes to the very core of musky fishing. And while it is easy to expound such a mantra from the comfort of a writing desk, it is quite different to live it in the elements that are faced during the course of a season. You must develop an approach to keep your head in the game. It may take some time to develop the confidence to work through the low points, but experience breeds the ability to stay positive when things aren't going particularly well. Knowing that there is always a reward for those who persist in the game of musky fishing will be the motivating factor.

Musky fishing should be viewed over a longer time period than just one day. Stepping back and analyzing a string of days will provide a greater perspective. By looking at a wider time frame, it is easy to see how short-term disappointments can be contributing factors to successful outings. Most anglers use the entire season to measure their success and reflect on the accomplishments. With this perspective the highs and lows are absorbed into one focused campaign.

While the mental aspect of this sport can be grueling, the physicality that it requires is also a consideration. Keeping yourself in good physical condition has many benefits, including being a key factor in musky fishing success. It allows you to work through the long days of repeated casts and standing in a boat. My regular trips to the gym condition my body to stay strong enough to cast to the very end. I want my outing to end because I ran out of water, time, or daylight, not because of fatigue. Keeping the body properly fueled and hydrated during an outing will help maintain a proper energy level and allow the mind to stay focused, while also enhancing the body's recovery time.

Being properly prepared also means being ready to make effective casts. This could be long casts to cover open water or short, precise casts to hit small pieces of structure. Casting practice is a must. You should regularly spend time maintaining or improving

Fishing with a good partner or guide can enhance the experience.

casting skills, but practice with a purpose. Lessons, books, and videos are all good sources to develop and improve skills. Always practice with a hookless fly similar in size and style to those normally used when musky fishing. Practice will not only improve distance and accuracy, but will also build endurance.

Proper preparation also extends to spending some time at the fly-tying bench or workbench to ensure proper rigging and to have a sufficient selection of flies. It may be part of maturity, but I find myself putting much more effort into this aspect in recent years, leaving nothing to chance when it comes to having the right lines, leaders, and flies to match the water I will be fishing. Fishing time is too valuable a commodity to waste an opportunity by not having the right tackle to meet the challenges of the day.

Being fully prepared for some types of fly fishing can be a daunting task, but it's fairly simple for musky. A small collection of fly lines will meet most musky-fishing situations, and an inventory of two or three types of leader material can be used to construct the final connection. Although it is essential to have a selection of flies to meet a range of conditions, this can be accomplished with a dozen or less in various sizes and colors.

While fly fishing for musky can be a solitary pursuit, because of the common use of watercraft, an outing often consists of fishing with one or more other musky anglers. Fishing with the right people is an integral part of overall enjoyment and success. Good partners are those whom you will enjoy spending long hours with in the confined boundaries of a small boat. Being consistently in sync with each other in terms of water selection and approach will enhance the fishing effort. Being on the some page allows each member of the party to fish with a purpose and patience.

A good partner is there to encourage and commiserate when times are low and share in the success when things are going well. This includes a healthy exchange of ideas on every aspect of the sport throughout the year. A good partner is one that you enjoy seeing catch a musky almost as much as if you were landing it yourself.

The aspect of finding the right people also extends to fishing with a guide. You need have a comfortable relationship that allows you to stay relaxed and in the zone during the outing. And it is important for the guide to feel that comfort level in order to make recommendations during the day that will increase your odds and enhance the overall experience.

Musky fishing isn't always a grueling experience. When the conditions are right, success in terms of landed fish can easily occur. But even when conditions stack up, consistent success will generally be reserved for those prepared to play. Always be ready—you never know when the next encounter will occur.

In the end, it is the mystique of *Esox masquinongy* that brings most of us to the water and fuels the madness. The unknown lurking beneath the surface draws us with the hope or even promise that we will experience an up-close meeting with this mighty predator. Success in the musky game is sweet, especially when shared with others that you respect and enjoy spending time with on the water. It is a feeling that every serious fly angler should experience in his or her lifetime.

3 RIGGED AND READY

Every form of fly fishing has certain requirements regarding equipment and rigging. Fly fishing for musky is certainly no exception. The challenge of equipment selection is complicated by the variety of casts and techniques needed to cover the range of waters that musky inhabit. Casting distance and accuracy while using a big, bushy fly is the top consideration, but fly depth, action, and being able to control the fly close to the boat is equally important.

Brad Bohen readies his rods and reels for the upcoming day.

This chapter will explore all aspects of equipment and rigging to successfully fly fish for musky, including a discussion of reels, rods, lines, leaders, and knots.

Reels

A number of characteristics go into a good musky fly reel. Despite the musky's fierce nature and potential size, a fight with one of these mighty fish can result in more of a tug-of-war and test of wills. This calls for a smooth, adjustable drag that can be tightened down to allow for a significant bend in the rod during a fight. It is critical to keep tight to the fish during the entire battle, but the drag should have low startup inertia that allows a musky to take line when needed. Often a fight with a musky is handled without ever getting the loose line caused by stripping the fly back onto the reel. In this situation the drag never comes into play. You keep the fish tight by continuing to strip line behind where it is pinched off against the rod handle.

Some rod manufacturers are producing fly rods specifically for musky hunting.

A good musky reel should have the capacity to handle a sufficient amount of 30-pound backing and 10-weight fly line. I prefer a large arbor reel for its capacity and its ability to pick up line. Line pickup is important when there is the opportunity during the fight to recover the stripped line onto the reel. While greater control of the fight and tension on the fish can often be maintained by stripping line and not using the reel, gathering the loose line eliminates the possibility of the line wrapping around a body part, the rod, or other obstruction. If fighting a fish from the reel, line pickup is also important for keeping tight to the fish when it makes an abrupt change in direction.

A musky reel must also balance well with the rod while the line is extended through the guides. A reel that is too heavy or too light will exert extra stress on the wrist, forearm, and elbow during an all-day outing. When the rod is held loosely by the handle or balanced on one finger, it should maintain a position parallel to the ground or water.

Reel durability also plays an important role. Most musky fly fishing will be done from a watercraft, and while some boats and personal craft have safe storage for rods and reels, many do not. Reels are subject to many abuses, both in use and while being stored. Using a solid reel will pay off over the course of a season. One of the disadvantages of some of the lighter reels on the market is that weight can be traded for durability.

Rods

Fly rods for musky can be called upon to perform a range of tasks, and it may be difficult to meet all the demands with just one rod. Some key considerations are casting distance, accuracy on shorter casts, the ability to lift bulky flies out of the water, and the ability to keep the fly swimming close to the boat, and they will vary by water type. Casting distance will be much more important when fishing lakes and larger rivers, while accuracy will be a key characteristic when fishing smaller musky rivers.

Nick Pionessa makes an effortless overhead cast with a two-handed rod.

The most useful rods in general for musky fly fishing are built for 9- through 11-weight lines. An 8-weight would be considered light in most situations but can be a useful tool on smaller rivers and creeks by providing acute line control in tight casting situations. The standard length of a typical musky rod is 9 feet. Single-hand rods up to 10 feet can also be used, though some anglers feel that this length is a bit cumbersome to maneuver close to the boat. Some 9- and 10-weight rods are only 8 feet long, a length that has some advantages while working the rod in close. I prefer this length rod when working tight structure on a small river, but the shorter length makes distance casting more challenging and reduces the depth the fly can be presented close to the boat.

The flex or action of the rod is an important consideration, and the type of water and casting requirements will factor heavily in the selection process. For making long casts with heavy sinking-tip shooting-head-style lines, I prefer a slightly slower-action rod that bends deep into the butt section. This action can efficiently launch the line and a big fly for significant distances when combined with a double haul. Faster-action rods excel at line pickup and are capable of creating tight casting loops with weight-forward tapers. This can be an advantage when making precise casts to specific structure such as a downed tree or fitting a cast into a tight spot under overhanging brush.

The rod's ability to work the fly close to the boat is a key consideration. A rod with a stiffer tip section will allow for more acute movement of the fly after the retrieve. Effectively working the fly close to the boat can result in a take from a fish visibly following the fly or one that is lazily hanging back out of sight. I prefer a rod with an oversize tip guide to allow the leader and junction with the fly line to easily slide in and out when working the fly close to the rod tip. I also prefer a rod with an oversize or extended butt section to easily accommodate the use of two hands while performing a boat-side figure eight.

The actual weight of the rod and balance in the angler's hand is also an important consideration. A day on the water may require casting for 6, 8, or even 10 hours. A rod that feels good in the hand is less fatiguing and will be more effective merely by being able to place the fly in the water for a longer period of time. The current market trend is to use the latest technology to produce lighter rods for 9- to 11-weight lines. Some fly rods on the market are designed specifically for musky fishing. The best musky fly rods combine a lighter weight with the ability of the rod to flex and launch long casts while being stiff enough to work the fly close in with the rod tip.

A switch rod is designed to be cast with either one hand or two. Generally, switch rods have a length of 10½ to 11½ feet with an extended butt section. While this length can be cumbersome around the boat, switch rods provide advantages that some musky fly fishers will find useful. Shorter two-handed rods can also be used for musky fishing. Overhead casting using two hands reduces the strain on the wrist, arm, and shoulder often experienced when single-hand casting for long periods of time. Two-hand casting can also make lighter work of casting large, wind-resistant flies and heavy sinking-tips for deeper water. And while the length of the rod is more difficult to maneuver around the boat, when the tip is pushed into the water, the fly can maintain a greater depth near the boat while performing a figure eight or sweeping presentation. A fly that is kept farther away from the boat seems to result in more takes.

Matching the proper line for the requirements of specific water will have a direct impact on fly presentation.

Lines

Muskies can be found in a wide range of habitats. Presenting a fly to all the places muskies live requires a repertoire of fly lines. If you fish mainly on one body of water, it may not be necessary to cover all the bases. But understanding how a line impacts fishing efficiency and presentation will improve your chances of a musky encounter.

While a full floating line may have limited application on some waters, every musky fly fisher should carry one in their gear bag. Floating lines for musky fishing should have a short, exaggerated forward taper that is capable of delivering large, bushy flies and are usually marketed as a musky/pike taper or some similar denotation. Floating lines are best suited to fishing surface flies or fishing weighted flies in shallow water.

The slow sink of an intermediate line can be useful in fairly shallow waters where you want the fly fished below the surface but not so deep that it hangs up on shallow bars and points. An intermediate line can also be used to fish a surface fly, as the line will pull the fly under the surface with each strip and then pop back to the surface on the pause. This approach is often more effective than simply fishing a fly on the surface. An effective intermediate line for musky fishing has an aggressive front taper and, like the floating line, may be marketed as a musky/pike taper. The color of the line should be natural to create an undetected approach, and some are even available in a camouflage design for the ultimate in stealthy presentation. Musky tapers are also available with medium to fast sinking-tip sections that can take the fly to substantial depths, making this a versatile line for both rivers and lakes.

The style of line that seems to have the widest application in musky fly fishing is a 24- to 30-foot shooting head sinking-tip. The tip section is slightly tapered, and the best-performing lines are density compensated for a uniform sink. This line style relies on a long running line section to propel the fly significant distances. A short rear taper provides a smooth transition from the tip to the running line to reduce any hinging effect during the cast. These lines have a rapid sink rate in the range of 7 to 9 inches per second and will often be denoted by the grain weight of the head as opposed to line weight. A 350- to 450-grain line matches up well with a 9- or 10-weight rod. A tip as heavy as 500 grains can be managed with a 10-weight as well and can be used to reach significant depths.

The shooting head sinking-tip line is versatile. Though able to cover depths of over 15 feet, with a fairly rapid retrieve this style of line can be used effectively in just a couple of feet of water. The shooting head aspect of the line allows it to load quickly for the next cast so that the fly is only out of the water for a short period of time. This line is available with both a floating running line or an intermediate running line option. The intermediate option allows the tip to attain great depths and remain deeper in the water column throughout the retrieve. The running line should maintain a low memory even in coldwater or cold weather conditions. Cast after cast must be completed without the running line coiling and causing tangles and knots during the retrieve and casting process. For this reason some musky anglers are turning to lines that are engineered for coldwater fishing for striped bass in the Northeast.

Other lines are available on the market that can effectively deliver a musky fly, but the best musky lines have similar characteristics: a short, aggressive weight-forward design with a low-memory running line capable of developing significant line speed and shooting long distances. A floating or intermediate line can be converted into a sinking-tip by adding a short section of fast-sink-rate material such as LC-13 or T-14 using a loop-to-loop connection. The extra sink created by the added tip can take the fly deep enough to elicit a strike where a floating or intermediate line would have fished the fly too high in the water column. Adding short tips seems to work best on small rivers and creeks. Sinking-tips can also be spliced to floating or intermediate lines for specific situations. Splicing creates a smoother transition than a loop connection and allows the line to pass more easily through the guides.

A deep running sinking-tip with a floating or intermediate running line is a versatile tool for musky fishing. JACK HANRAHAN PHOTO

Many of the lines manufactured for switch rods are designed for Spey casting or delivering smaller flies with an overhead cast. It may take some trial and error to find the right line to deliver a big musky fly, but a key consideration is the grain weight of the head. Generally an 8- or 9-weight switch or two-handed rod will require a line that has a head of a greater grain weight than an 8- or 9-weight single-handed rod. Short-head lines designed to throw heavy tips work well with a switch or two-hand rod. Lines designed for interchangeable tips create a versatile setup that can be quickly adjusted to meet various conditions.

An effective line for two-handed overhead casting can easily be constructed with a 25- to 30-foot section of sinking line such as T-11, T-14, or even T-17 and running line. The two lines can be joined using a loop-to-loop connection by folding over the ends of each line and securing the loop with a fly-tying bobbin and a heavy tying thread. Braided loop connectors can also be used to join two lines using a loop-to-loop connection; the braided material slips over the line and can be secured with monofilament and a nail knot. However, the smoothest connection point for drawing the line through the guides during the retrieve involves creating a more permanent bond. This can be done by stripping the sinking line down to its core and then connecting it to the running line using an Albright knot. A piece of shrink tubing can then be used to further smooth out the connection point. Another permanent connection method is to use a hollow braided running line and run the hollow end of the braid onto the sinking line. The running line can then be secured with monofilament and a nail knot or with shrink tubing.

The homemade shooting head line can also be used effectively with a single-hand rod, though a slight hinging effect may occur at the connection point since there is no taper at the rear of the sinking section. However, the line speed generated with this type of shooting head line provides good water coverage because few false casts are required. This approach also provides for versatility, as custom lines can be created cost-effectively for covering specific situations.

Leaders

Leaders for musky fishing are generally not complicated. An effective leader has three main characteristics. First, it needs to efficiently transfer energy in order to turn over big, bushy flies with every cast. Second, the leader should be constructed in a manner that allows it to slide easily through the guides of the rod since the fly will be drawn within a few feet of the rod tip on almost every retrieve. And third, an effective musky leader must have a bite guard to protect against the extremely sharp teeth that fill the mouth of a mature *Esox*.

Musky leaders can be fairly simple but must be carefully constructed.

Nate Carr used a single strand wire bite guard to land this stout tiger musky. NATE CARR PHOTO

A butt section created with 40- to 50-pound-test monofilament with a diameter of .025 to .030 inch will provide the backbone to transition the energy of the cast down to the fly. The butt section should be constructed from a fairly stiff material that will create fly turnover on every cast. Fluorocarbon is typically used for the butt section since this material is stiff and isn't as visible in the water as standard monofilament.

Fly-fishing leaders for big fish typically have a class tippet in the middle constructed of 12- to 30-pound-test material, usually fluorocarbon. The class tippet provides the measuring point for world-record catches and adds an element of stealth to the presentation, though this effect is minimized because a bite guard is required on musky leaders before the fly is attached. The class tippet also provides a breaking point in the event the fly and leader become entangled in an obstruction in the water, which can occur with or without a fish attached to the fly. A breaking point in the leader can save a fly line or release a fish if it gets caught in a deep-water snag. Being able to break the leader can also mitigate a dangerous situation, such as attempting to remove a fly from a snag in faster current.

The class tippet can be added to the butt section with a handful of knots that connect two pieces of monofilament. The double surgeon's knot provides a strong, easy-to-tie connection for two pieces of leader that are close in diameter. The Albright knot is an effective connection for pieces of leader material that have a large difference in diameter, and since the disparity between the butt section and class tippet is usually fairly significant, the Albright is commonly used by musky fly fishers. While this knot seems cumbersome to tie, with practice it is actually quite simple and can easily be performed on the water when the need arises. Another effective knot for attaching two pieces of leader material is the easy to tie, low-profile slim beauty. Adding knot sealer to this connection will help it flow through the guides at the end of the retrieve.

The next section of the leader is the bite guard, which is generally between 1 and 2 feet in length and constructed of either wire or a thick-diameter fluorocarbon. It is nearly impossible for the sharp teeth of a musky to cut through quality wire, and this is its main advantage as a leader material.

Single-strand stainless wire provides the most basic approach. Loops can be created at both ends of the wire using a knot such as the haywire twist, and the wire can be attached to the monofilament section of the leader using a loop-to-loop connection. Single-strand wire in the 80- to 100-pound-test range provides enough strength and flexibility in the water; dark or camouflage styles create an element of stealth.

Another option is to use wire that is flexible enough to allow for conventional knots. Knotable wire has properties similar to stiff, heavy monofilament. This type of bite guard material is made with a core of flexible, thin strands of wire covered with a nylon coating. The wire can be twisted and turned to form knots, and the coating creates a base that keeps the knot from slipping. Knotable wire should have at least a 25- to 30-pound break strength for musky. It can be attached to the monofilament leader using a double surgeon's knot or by forming a perfection loop or surgeon's loop and attaching the end of each material using a loop-to-loop connection.

Heavy fluorocarbon provides a bite guard option that is considered the stealthiest approach since this material is less visible in the water. The hard nature of fluorocarbon reduces the possibility of sharp edges cutting through the material, and a fluorocarbon bite guard will knot to the class tippet using a double surgeon's knot, Albright knot, or a two-turn versus four-turn uni knot. But a fluorocarbon bite guard is not 100 percent effective. In fact, almost every serious musky fisher that has used fluorocarbon for any length of time has a story that ends badly with a sliced bite tippet caused by a musky's sharp teeth. To make matters worse, it is usually the bigger fish that slice the fluorocarbon bite guard.

However, not all fluorocarbon materials are created equal. Carefully selecting the material for a bite guard will dramatically reduce the chance of a bite-off. The most effective material has a diameter of at least .035 inch and an overall stiff consistency. The thicker diameter allows for some nicks in the fluorocarbon from the teeth of a musky while continuing to maintain its strength. The overall stiffness or hardness makes it more difficult to cut the material. Much of the fluorocarbon on the market is designed for tying knots easily and may be too soft for an effective bite guard.

In a day and age when the angler's concern for the valuable musky resource is at an all-time high, the chance of leaving a big hook and 12 inches of fly or lure in a fish's mouth is something that should be avoided. Personally, I have moved toward using wire for my bite guard. While I do think fluorocarbon has a stealth and tactical advantage in certain situations, musky are generally not leader-shy. Once a musky locks in on a fly, the type of bite guard does not seem to have a significant impact on whether the fish will commit to a take.

Manufactured leaders for toothy critters are available in various lengths. These leaders generally have a tapered rear section of fluorocarbon or standard monofilament with a bite guard of wire, titanium, or heavy fluorocarbon knotted or integrated into the leader. There will usually be a loop on the butt end for an easy loop-to-loop connection to the fly line. Some manufactured leaders for toothy fish have a barrel swivel or snap swivel integrated into the bite guard. A stout snap swivel can be added to the barrel swivel. While a swivel at the end of the bite tippet adds a cumbersome aspect to the leader, it also facilitates quick fly changes, particularly in cold-weather conditions. Heavy snap swivels can be added to homemade leaders as well and can be an advantage when fishing areas that require frequent fly changes. Make sure the swivel is constructed in a way that it won't fail if connected to the fish of a lifetime.

Leaders generally vary in length from 5 to 9 feet. Longer leaders will match up best with floating and intermediate lines, while shorter leaders are best suited for sinking-tips. The proportions of a typical 6-foot sinking-tip leader will generally be 2½ feet of butt section, 2 feet of class tippet, and 18 to 24 inches of bite guard. To lengthen this basic leader, the butt section can simply be extended. Specific minimum lengths for the class tippet and maximum length for the bite guard apply when in pursuit of an International Game Fish Association (IGFA) world record, so it is important to consult the current rules before rigging up.

Knots and connection points are inherent in all fly-fishing rigging systems, but when rigging for

Blane Chocklett and Brad Bohen discuss leader construction before heading to the water.

musky, the connection points can be more cumbersome because of the heavy butt section typically used for the leader. Because the most effective retrieve for musky will draw the fly within 1 to 2 feet of the rod tip, it is imperative that the connection between the fly line and leader slide easily into the tip-top guide.

The butt section can be attached to the fly line using a double nail knot; this connection is strong and fairly low-profile. Another option is to use an Albright knot. However, my preferred connection is to create a loop at the end of the fly line by doubling over the last inch of the tip and lashing it down on itself with 6/0 or 3/0 tying thread. The connection is completed with a flexible cement or knot sealer. Either a perfection loop or surgeon's loop can be created at the end of the butt section and connected to the fly line using a loop-to-loop connection. A perfection loop creates a smaller knot than a surgeon's loop, resulting in a lower-profile connection. The connection between the knot and fly line can be made smoother by covering it with heat-shrink tubing, but make sure the fly line or leader material is not heated to the point of compromising its strength. The connection can also be covered with a UV knot coating or with Clear Cure Goo to create a smooth surface that moves easily through the guides.

For quick fly changes, attach a class tippet and bite guard to each of your favorite patterns. With a perfection loop at the rear end of the class tippet, this section of leader can easily be added to the butt section through a loop-to-loop connection. The perfection loop at the end of the butt section needs to be large enough to pass over the entire fly to complete the connection. The section of leader attached to the fly can be neatly coiled in a fly box or stored using a box or board that keeps the class tippet and bite guard stretched out and ready to use. In addition to providing for a quick fly change, having the class tippet and bite guard attached maintains a consistent bite guard length and eliminates the chance of tying a poor knot due to adverse weather conditions or being in a hurry.

A simple leader of 30-pound fluorocarbon and knotable wire was used to fool my personal best musky.

Knots tied carefully under the controlled conditions of a fly-tying bench are more likely to result in a solid, effective connection.

A simple musky leader can be created using a single piece of non-tapered 30- to 40-pound fluorocarbon approximately 4 to 6 feet in length to turn over the fly. The main advantage of this design is that it eliminates the knots within the main portion of the leader, allowing it to readily slide through the guides. The disadvantage is that there is no easy break point in the leader. A perfection loop is used to attach the leader to the fly line with a loop-to-loop connection. A large perfection or surgeon's loop is formed at the other end to connect the wire bite guard. The wire bite guard of either single-strand or knotable wire is added using a loop-to-loop connection. The loop at the end of the monofilament should be large enough to fit over a fly so that pattern changes can be made quickly at the point between the leader and bite guard. By keeping a preferred length of bite guard attached to each fly, changes can quickly be made without altering the length of the components of the leader.

This is my preferred leader rig due to its simplicity and consistency in component length. With a smooth connection between the fly line and fluorocarbon, the knot between the monofilament and bite guard creates the first resistance point in the retrieve and signifies the time to stop retrieving and begin a figure eight movement.

The knot between the bite guard and the fly can represent a slight challenge. For single-strand wire, the material can be threaded through the eyelet of the fly before forming the haywire twist. Alternatively a split ring and heavy snap swivel can be used to connect the fly to the wire; this method allows for a quick change and additional movement of the fly. The Homer Rhode loop knot or nonslip loop knot can be tied with knotable wire or fluorocarbon. A three- or four-turn improved clinch knot also creates a secure connection when using knotable wire. A two-turn uni knot creates a secure connection when using stiff fluorocarbon.

Since all the knots in a musky leader will be constructed with thick, stiff monofilament and/or wire, care must be taken in tying each and every one. Make sure to lubricate each knot thoroughly before tightening—it is critical that the knot is properly seated so that it doesn't slip or unravel. Pliers should be used to grasp the tag end of the knot and tighten firmly with a slow, steady pull. A connection between two stout pieces of monofilament can easily fail with a sloppy knot. Every hookup with a musky is an accomplishment. So many things can go wrong, but losing a fish over a poor knot should never happen.

As evidenced above, numerous alternatives and combinations exist for creating an effective musky leader. There is certainly no one right way, as most anglers have their own twist on the composition of a musky leader. Choices are made based on conditions and general fishing style or preference. My own preference is for simplicity, tending toward a leader arrangement with a minimum of knots that can easily and quickly be tied on the water.

Watercraft

While targeting musky offers plenty of wading and shoreline fishing opportunities, the use of a watercraft opens up much more area to fish with a fly. Watercraft also allows an angler to cover a variety of structure from a position that will best present the fly.

A detailed coverage of boat options for musky fly fishing could fill its own book. There are so many good products on the market today that the key lies in finding the craft that best matches the water that you regularly fish. This section of the book looks at a handful of choices available for various types of musky water.

A craft does not have to be expensive, and plenty of options in the personal watercraft category can be

A drift boat is perfect for covering rivers of nearly any size.

A skiff is a versatile vessel that can also be outfitted with a small motor.

successfully used for musky. Kayaks and pontoon-type craft can both be effective for covering smaller, quieter waters. A personal craft that you can stand in provides a significant advantage, as standing allows for an effective figure eight movement at the end of the retrieve and the ability to see if a fish is following the fly as it draws close to the craft. Some kayak designs allow an angler to comfortably stand while fishing. A pontoon boat with a floor allows you to stand with a bit more stability. An advantage to these smaller craft is the ability to launch nearly anywhere.

For floating a river between two points, a drift boat or multiple-person raft can be a great musky craft. A good drift boat is stable and provides enough room for loose line created by retrieving the fly. It can also be maneuvered in tight areas and cover specific structure. Stable hybrid-type skiffs are also popular for drifting musky water and generally provide for even more fishing room than a drift boat. Two- or three-person rafts are stable and can be used to cover a variety of water. The tubes of the raft can make working the fly near the boat somewhat cumbersome, however, and a raft does not maneuver as easily as a drift boat or skiff. But rafts are a lower-cost option that can be launched in places where a boat cannot. There are also a number of lightweight two-man raft options on the market that are perfect for stealth and getting into tight places. All of these watercraft can be rigged with an electric motor or even a very light gas engine to cover small lakes or to make it back up a river.

When fishing bigger waters, I prefer a motorized boat. A 16- to 20-foot craft will fish two anglers comfortably. A smaller boat will also work fine on lakes and rivers without a lot of boat traffic.

The most important elements are that the craft be stable and comfortable for fishing. The best boats for musky angling have a raised deck in the front and back to provide a higher vantage point for looking into the water. The higher angle gives you the advantage of seeing if there is any activity behind your fly. A good musky boat should also have at least a modest amount of electronics. An electric motor mounted on the bow allows for boat control and covering specific structure. One with foot controls or that can be programmed keeps the hands free for fishing. A graph that denotes depth and bottom contour is critical for finding sunken structure.

A motorized boat can be outfitted with a standard propeller drive or a jet drive. The propeller is a basic way to cover open-water lakes and big rivers. The jet drive is perfect for areas with a widely uneven bottom where structure can be within inches of the surface. A jet drive will also work well on shallow rivers or reservoirs where sunken timber is found near the surface.

A key element of any musky craft is that it remains relatively free from obstructions that can catch line while casting or when a fish is hooked. Line catchers should be removed or covered to reduce or eliminate this occurrence. Every boat should have a system for keeping loose clothing or tackle away from coils of line. A dry bag or cooler can be used on craft with limited designated storage areas.

When it comes to watercraft keep an open mind. A large investment is often not necessary. Inexpensive older craft can be modified to meet the demands of local waters. Adding casting decks to an old row or johnboat can create a musky chasing machine that can meet a wide range of water types. I had years of service from an inexpensive aluminum boat that I modified with the help of my dad that allowed me to pursue musky on waters big and small.

It is very important to fish from an area that is free of items that can catch and tangle loose line.

NICK PIONESSA PHOTO

4 MAKING THE CAST

Consistently delivering the fly to areas where a musky may be lurking starts with the cast. Making and repeating the same cast throughout the day is the key to effectively covering as much water as possible. The larger, wind-resistant flies that are normally used to fool a musky add to the challenge of casting. The key is to develop a sound casting technique that uses an efficient series of motions. Being able to create sufficient line speed and a tight casting loop will result in both distance and accuracy.

A smooth, tight loop creates the most efficient cast. NICK PIONESSA PHOTO

Developing good casting fundamentals is the key to delivering big, wind-resistant flies. NICK PIONESSA PHOTO

Distance casting can be very important when covering open water. With the equipment and instructional information available today, most anglers should be able to make casts of 70 feet or more. But even more important than sheer distance is developing a casting routine that results in consistency. An effective cast for musky fishing is one delivered with enough energy so that the leader straightens out entirely with no slack in the line or leader.

Accuracy can be more important than distance on some water. Dropping a cast alongside a logjam or downed tree will often be the key to triggering a fish to eat. There may also be the need to fit a cast precisely between the branches of two bankside trees or even under overhanging branches and vines. While a musky will often move a fair distance to ambush a fly, minute of angle accuracy is normally not required. But the ability to place the fly consistently in a desired spot will pay big dividends over the course of a day or a season.

The Basics

Developing good casting fundamentals is the only approach for making consistent casts. An understanding of the fundamentals leads to versatility and the ability to troubleshoot when casting results are not meeting expectations.

When making a cast with a musky fly, I focus on a few key steps. The rod should be moved in a smooth accelerating motion and come to an abrupt and definite stop at the end of the stroke. In other words, the rod should go from a stopped position to moving at its fastest pace just prior to another firm stop. This motion literally throws the line, and when the acceleration is smooth, the line will be straight and devoid of shockwaves that steal momentum from the line.

I attempt to create both the back and forward cast with a tight loop that has the appearance of a wedge as it travels through the air. The distance the rod tip drops during the acceleration to the point of the next stop determines the size of the casting loop. The less the tip drops, the tighter the casting loop, and vice versa. As the tip travels through the casting motion, I try to draw a straight line that is basically parallel to the water's surface. You can also think of the rod movement in terms of the arc or angle as it moves through the casting stroke. A tighter angle or arc results in a tighter casting loop, where a more open movement or arc results in a larger, less efficient loop creating less momentum in the line.

Moving the rod tip in a straight plane toward the target during the acceleration and stop of the forward delivery allows the fly to turn over straight as it hits the water. A fly flopping to one side or the other at the end of the cast is the result of the rod tip not moving in a straight plane prior to making a full stop. A rod movement over a longer distance during the back and forward cast allows it to operate at peak efficiency. This means moving the casting hand to the rear during the backcast and forward toward the target as the rod accelerates to an abrupt stop. The longer movement allows the rod to load deeply, creating more power and line speed. Developing line speed is critical when musky fishing. Most casts will be made with a relatively short head, and maximizing distance relies on shooting a substantial amount of line by building up speed.

Other essential considerations for the basic fly cast include grip and rod angle. The rod should be gripped

Cast, cast, cast—it's normally what it takes to catch a trophy like the one John Fabian is holding.
MIKE SCHULTZ PHOTO

Steve Wascher completes an accurate cast to some good-looking structure.

lightly with the thumb on top. Proper thumb positioning allows for maximum power during the acceleration phase of the cast. The amount of pressure applied with the grip on the rod should increase only toward the end of the acceleration at the point when maximum power is applied to the stroke. Gripping the rod too tightly throughout the entire cast is both tiring and disruptive to the cadence and rhythm of the cast. The hand will also experience cramping when gripping too tightly for extended periods of time. Cramping can also occur if the physical size of the grip on the rod does not match up with the size of your hand. Generally a larger hand will feel more comfortable with a grip that has a larger circumference. Locking the butt of the rod into the underside of the forearm creates a stronger grip and allows the rod to be a solid extension of the casting arm.

I prefer to keep the rod tip slightly angled away at about 30 to 45 degrees from my body during the cast. This positioning has a few advantages, the first being safety. The rod tip pointing slightly to the side keeps the line and fly with a 5/0 hook away from my body. This positioning also allows me to open up my body and make long, efficient strokes with the rod. Also, with the tip pointed off to the side, I can watch my line during the cast to make sure my timing is proper and to help deal with casting encumbrances like overhanging branches or windy conditions.

These basic principles should be incorporated into your casting style. The rigors and demands of casting a large, wind-resistant fly for hours on end require an efficient casting style that allows the rod to operate as a lever. Even accomplished casters can be challenged by the conditions or casting situations presented when musky fishing. Being able to make proper adjustments when on the water is extremely important.

Accuracy

Casting accuracy is most important when fishing rivers along specific structure or when covering weed edges and cuts in big, open water. Since most casts are made blindly, precise accuracy like that needed when fishing for selectively feeding trout or bonefish is generally not necessary, but the ability to consistently place the fly in an area that gives it the best chance to be seen by a musky is key. When drifting a river this includes being able to quickly judge distances and being aware of any casting obstructions as the boat moves with the current. Often you only get one good shot at a potential holding spot, so making the cast count will increase the odds in your favor.

The first step to accuracy is making a solid cast that allows the fly to turn over entirely and completely straighten out the leader. Make sure the rod tip moves in a straight line, with the tip pointing at the target when the forward cast is completed. The tip should act as a gun sight in lining up the cast. When casting from watercraft, the distance to the structure can change as you drift. I normally keep enough line stripped to make my longest cast. I can then adjust the distance by reducing the power on my forward stroke or grabbing the running line with my line hand as it shoots through the guides once I have judged that the fly has traveled the desired distance. Controlling the running line will be discussed in detail later in the chapter.

Getting the cast to go straight and in the desired direction is fairly easy with some practice, but judging distance can be tricky. Structure will often be located near or along shore. When fishing from watercraft and casting toward the bank, the casting length can remain fairly constant if the craft position is carefully maintained during the drift. However, it is important to constantly look for subtle changes in boat direction, contour of the shoreline, or angle of the structure so that adjustments to length can be factored into the next cast. I try to look one cast ahead, peeking downriver while midway through my retrieve. I don't want to rush my retrieve, since many fish are caught at the boat, but I also want to hit all the prime spots.

Sometimes getting the right distance comes down to judgment. Experience and time on the water can be the best tools for making a cast of the proper length. One approach I use to judge distance is to become familiar with the length of the head of the line I am using. The constant of the head length takes some of the guesswork out of calculating how much running line it will take to reach the desired structure. It is important to make a cast to the structure with

This fish was holding tightly to a logjam.

confidence. Continually placing the fly short of the target limits the opportunity to entice a musky. However, over-casting into the structure can disrupt the rhythm of the float and disturb potential holding water.

Overhanging structure provides its own set of challenges. Since this type of cover can provide fish with a certain level of security, it is important to develop an approach to cover this water. A standard cast will typically get caught in low overhanging branches as the casting loop unfolds and turns over but can fit under moderate overhang by simply adjusting the trajectory of the cast. Driving a tight loop of line down at the water will keep the line and fly fairly low, but fitting a cast under the lowest overhang requires changing the angle of the rod by nearly 90 degrees. The rod will then move nearly parallel to the water's surface as opposed to perpendicular. The casting principles remain the same, but the change in casting angle allows the line and fly to travel just a foot or two above the water's surface.

Accuracy isn't simply about making straight-line casts. Sometimes casting around structure provides the best presentation. Since the line will go in the direction of the rod, curving the path of the rod tip as the acceleration of the forward stroke is completed has the effect of curving the tip of the line. This can be a useful tactic when presenting to such areas as the backside of a downed tree lying partially submerged in the water or a small bay created by a point protruding into the river on a downriver angle. The rod tip should be moved in the direction of the desired curve by turning the wrist and forearm in a precise movement made at the very end of the forward stroke. An abrupt movement will normally work best, as this will cause the line to form more of a right angle, allowing the fly and last 10 or 20 feet of line and leader to flop to the left or right. Turn the wrist and forearm to the left to curve left and to the right to curve right.

Distance

Casting distance is most important when fishing open water on lakes and big rivers. Under these circumstances, longer casts mean more time in the water for the fly. And when fishing areas with depth, a longer cast allows the fly to get deeper and stay at that level of the water column for a prolonged period of time.

Casting for distance begins with developing and practicing good casting form. A smooth acceleration to a quick stop when making the back and forward cast should be the foundation of every cast. Pushing the rod too quickly at the beginning of the stroke creates shockwaves in the line and is an inefficient use of energy. Moving the rod over as long a distance as possible allows the rod to operate as an efficient lever.

I open up my body during the cast to allow the rod to move its greatest distance. As a right-handed caster, I place my left foot in front of my right. This allows me to rotate through the backcast and let my entire body become part of the casting motion. At the end of the backcast, my left shoulder is pointing at the target and my right arm is extended back. Through the forward stroke, my body rotates back toward the target with my shoulders ending square and right arm extended forward. This allows the rod to travel its maximum distance.

Maintaining a small or tight casting loop allows the line to knife through the air. Focus on the rod tip traveling in a fairly straight line relative to the water's surface. Moving the rod over a longer distance facilitates a tight loop by helping to avoid an open arc in the tip of the rod. A large arc in the rod tip is an inefficient movement that results in restricted line speed.

The essential element to distance casting is the haul. Every good distance caster includes this movement as part of his or her basic cast. The haul is a downward movement with the line hand that is applied during the acceleration of the casting stroke. When applied at the precise time toward the end of the stroke, the haul significantly increases line speed by placing a deeper load into the rod. I apply the haul with an accelerating downward movement of the line hand just as the stroke is completed and prior to the abrupt stop of the rod. To incorporate this motion at the proper time takes practice, but with repetition it should become a standard part of every cast.

It is actually the double haul that maximizes line speed when casting. The double haul is simply the standard haul on both the back and forward cast. Adding the haul to the backcast allows the rod to load deeply and set up a forward cast that will carry the momentum of the extra rod flex. The double haul should be used on all false casts prior to the cast that will deliver the fly to the water. The key to the double haul is getting the line hand back into position after making the first

Jay Nichols completes the perfect double haul.

Beginning the backcast with line hand near the stripping guide.

NICK PIONESSA PHOTO

Bringing the rod back while beginning the haul.

NICK PIONESSA PHOTO

Completing the backcast with a full haul on the line.

NICK PIONESSA PHOTO

The line hand returns to the position near the rod hand before beginning the forward stroke.
NICK PIONESSA PHOTO

Beginning the haul on the forward stroke accelerates the speed of the line. NICK PIONESSA PHOTO

The cast is completed with a full movement of the line hand to complete the haul. NICK PIONESSA PHOTO

haul. The haul is most efficient when it starts with the line hand positioned near the rod hand. When the haul is made on the backcast, the line hand must return to a position near the rod hand in order to complete the haul on the forward cast. This is accomplished by letting the line hand drift back at the end of the backcast. Actually, with a strong backcast the momentum of the line practically pulls the hand back into position and the second haul can then be applied as the forward cast is completed. The extra line speed that is gained through a properly utilized double haul is significant and is the key to shooting line. The double haul can add 30 feet or more to the cast.

Managing Line and Delivering a Cast

Because the fly will be stripped back to within a couple of feet of the boat after every cast, dealing with the loose line that has been retrieved is an essential part of making repeated casts. Loose running line becoming tangled or wrapped around objects can be the greatest source of frustration when musky fishing, but steps can be taken that result in consistent casts nearly every time.

When fishing from a boat or other watercraft, I strip the line onto the deck or floor. It is critical that your fishing area in the boat or craft be relatively free of obstructions that can tangle line. Nonessential items on a boat that continually catch line should be removed or modified. Loose running line will find every possible obstruction, so limiting as many as possible will go a long way toward efficient casting and reduced frustration. Keep your watercraft organized, and place extra tackle and clothing in storage.

Distance casting requires the ability to shoot all the line that is stripped out on the deck. Before each cast I check to make sure my running line is free and ready to shoot. When the air temperatures allow, I fish with no shoes or socks so that I can feel if the line is under my feet. This is especially helpful when making quick casts in various directions. A smooth acceleration

Line being stripped onto an open casting deck.

Joe Goodspeed caught this impressive musky using a water haul.

during false casting and when delivering the actual cast is key to an efficient cast and an important part of line management. A smooth casting style allows the line to flow through the guides and reduces the possibility of tangles.

When casting to structure, I sometimes maintain constant contact with the running line as it shoots through the guides by forming an O with the thumb and forefinger of my line hand. The O is formed at the completion of the double haul and effectively creates an additional line guide. While the O can create additional drag, it has the effect of smoothing out the running line as it shoots. The biggest advantage of this approach is that when the cast is complete, the line is already in the grip of the line hand and the retrieve and movement of the fly can begin immediately. This is important when making quick casts to specific holding areas. By maintaining constant contact with the line, you can easily shorten the cast midair by clamping down on the line. This can be useful if you calculate that the cast that has just been released is going to end up in the structure.

Allow line that has been stripped onto the deck to remain as undisturbed as possible. When it is stripped into a pile, the line that was last retrieved will be on top and in position to go smoothly back out first with the next cast. When the coils of line flip and move around, the chance for a tangle increases significantly. Be especially careful of this occurring when changing casting direction. The same principles apply when using a stripping basket; however, a basket will allow for easier change of directions.

A key element of line management is the readying of line to make the next cast. Since the typical retrieve will bring the fly within a couple feet of the rod with the leader inside the tip, enough line needs to be released past the tip to begin loading the rod for the next cast. Use the tension of the water to pull line past the tip. After completing a figure eight motion, I allow line to slip through where it is pinched off against the cork while moving my arm away from the fly and upward into a backcast position. Toward the end of this movement, I pinch off the line. With a

Starting the next cast by allowing the tension of the water to pull the connection of the line and leader past the rod tip. NICK PIONESSA PHOTO

The line and fly are pulled from the water with an accelerating movement of the rod and a haul with the line hand. NICK PIONESSA PHOTO

The backcast is completed with a full haul by the line hand and allowing some line to slip through to lengthen the line beyond the tip. NICK PIONESSA PHOTO

The line hand drifts back to the rod hand before starting the forward stroke. NICK PIONESSA PHOTO

The first false cast is completed with the tip or head of the line all sliding beyond the rod tip.
NICK PIONESSA PHOTO

wide, accelerating movement of the rod, I can get the leader and enough line past the tip to load the rod for a short false cast.

I use the first full false cast to allow more line to slip through my line hand on both the back and forward casting motion. Ideally, when the first full false cast is complete, the head of the fly line will be positioned just outside of the tip of the rod. Allowing the head to move past the tip actually takes some finesse. The head of the line will usually be fairly heavy and build momentum quickly. A smooth, controlled false cast is all that is needed to get the head beyond the rod. A smooth motion is the key, since an erratic movement can cause the running line to jump up quickly and cause a tangle. It is best to use a line that has a dramatic change in color from the head to the running line to see when the line is properly positioned past the tip.

The next false cast should be used to make any adjustments to the positioning of the line head so that it is properly lined up for the cast while getting your body lined up and in rhythm with the rod and line. The third false cast is used to impart momentum to the line with a smooth acceleration and a well-timed double haul. The cast is then delivered with an abrupt stop, allowing the stripped running line to flow through the guides of the rod. I will often make an extra false cast to assure that I have the proper rhythm to generate sufficient line speed to complete the desired cast.

When fishing smaller rivers from a drifting boat, it is usually more effective to make quick accurate casts to specific structure. In this situation I attempt to make a cast with only two false casts by trying to get most of the head of the line past the rod tip on the first false cast and using the next false cast to deliver the line.

An alternative to beginning the first false cast by pulling the fly into the air is to simply roll the tip of the line onto the water's surface. Once the figure eight is completed, the tension of the water is used to pull the leader and line past the tip. At the same time the rod is raised to the 12 o'clock position with an accelerated movement. A forward, accelerated motion of the rod completes the roll cast. As the line touches the water's surface, it is picked up quickly before it begins to sink. The tension of the line and fly on the surface loads the rod for the backcast portion of the first false. You may find rolling the line onto the water's surface makes it easier to begin the casting process. However, this approach may not be as stealthy. When fishing with another angler in the boat, I try to keep disturbance on the water to a minimum because this can potentially spook a fish that has followed my partner's retrieve to the boat. I'm not sure if this is a significant concern, since musky are so inconsistent with their behavior, but my stealthy nature as a fly fisher tells me that keeping a low profile may be preferred.

The water haul is an adaptation to the standard cast that loads the rod by allowing the line and fly to contact the water's surface. By waiting at the end of the backcast for the line to drop and briefly come in contact with the water, the rod loads deeply to propel a forceful forward cast. This cast is accomplished by rolling the line forward to get it started and then allowing most or all of the head of the line to release past the tip on the backcast. Just as the line touches the water's surface, a forward stroke with a smooth acceleration and a single haul completes the cast.

The water haul is also useful for making quick casts to structure, since false casting is all but eliminated. It is also a good approach when casting double-handed with a switch rod. Allowing the fly and head of the line to touch as the forward stroke begins loads the rod deep and creates a similar feel as when making a Spey cast. This can be a very effective cast when using a switch or even a full two-handed rod. The water haul is best used when both anglers are fishing out of the same side of the boat, since the line and fly's contact with the water creates a significant disturbance that could spook a musky. When using a single-handed rod, I prefer the standard cast to the water haul for its distance and accuracy. However, the water haul is essential for any musky angler's arsenal when delivering a fly and works especially well when handling heavy, bulky flies.

Making Adjustments

Real fishing situations commonly require adjustments. While making the perfect cast might be the goal every time you pick up a fly rod, weather conditions and the demands of covering certain holding structure can make that nearly impossible. It won't always be pretty, but persevering and producing casts that are as good as can be given the conditions is part of musky fishing. Making consistent casts regardless of the conditions will provide the best odds. And the stronger your casting skills, the better equipped you will be for facing adverse circumstances.

When fishing from a boat, wind is the enemy of a musky fly fisher and the source of a number of challenges to overcome. Gusty winds make it difficult to strip line onto the deck during the retrieve. Wind can also disrupt the line that has already been retrieved, causing frustrating tangles. Stripping the line onto the lower deck or actually fishing from the lower deck will sometimes provide sufficient protection, but for heavy, persistent winds, stripping the line into a cylinder to gain protection from the wind is the best approach. There are cylinders on the market produced specifically for this purpose, or you can improvise using a bucket or expandable clothes hamper. An expandable cylinder can be conveniently stored when not in use. It may take some time getting used to a cylinder since you have to make sure that all the stripped-in line lands inside in the order it is retrieved. But with the aggravation that using a cylinder can save, it is well worth the effort of focusing on the stripped line. A stripping basket is another tool for managing loose line. While a basket can be used when fishing from a boat, I find it restricts my retrieve too much. But stripping baskets are useful when fishing from a canoe or kayak or when wading in musky water.

The wind not only wreaks havoc on loose line, but also creates difficulties when delivering a cast with a big, air-resistant fly. Using the lee of a shoreline can take the bite of the wind. Also, positioning the boat

The wind can create certain challenges when musky fishing with a fly.

so that the wind is at your back can make it more tolerable. However, when drifting a winding river, you are mainly at the wind's mercy. Casting into the wind requires a tight casting loop and good line speed while maintaining a casting angle that is pointed at the water's surface. The strength of the wind is often lowest near the surface of the water. Allowing the line to travel in a low trajectory allows for less impact of the wind. Casting in the wind may require you to shorten the length of the cast. I think it is best to select a cast length that is comfortable for the conditions and can be repeated throughout the day.

Casting in the wind isn't all about effectiveness, but also about safety. Anytime there are 5/0 hooks zipping through the air at high speed there should be cause for concern. The most dangerous situation is caused by wind blowing onto the casting shoulder. This should be avoided by boat positioning when possible, but when this doesn't fix the problem, adjustments can be made to the standard cast to improve safety. One approach is to keep the line low and well off to the side, and this works well for a moderate-strength wind. For more fierce gusts, I will lift the rod high and go right overhead. With this approach it is essential that you maintain a strong backcast that angles the fly up and well above your head. You won't get the same distance with either of these adjustments, but it is a good trade-off for safety. I often use the water haul in extreme or swirling winds, especially when the direction of the wind is pushing into my casting position. Eliminating the false casting of the standard cast creates a safer environment in these conditions.

When fishing from a boat, you must remain flexible with your casting. It may not be possible to cover the best target with a standard forward cast. You may need to utilize your backcast, which will significantly increase the amount of water that you can cover. Also, when two anglers with the same dominant hand are

To deliver the fly with the backcast start with a haul on the forward stroke. NICK PIONESSA PHOTO

Allow the line hand to drift up to the rod at the end of the stroke. NICK PIONESSA PHOTO

Make the backstroke with a haul and body opened to up toward the target. NICK PIONESSA PHOTO

Make an abrupt stop with the rod to throw the line in a tight loop.
NICK PIONESSA PHOTO

Allow the line to shoot through the guides assisting with an "O" in the line hand if necessary.
NICK PIONESSA PHOTO

fishing from a boat covering the same shoreline, one will need to present the fly on his or her backcast to avoid casting through the middle of the vessel.

The backcast can be as powerful as a standard forward cast. Actually, the backcast is just the reverse, or mirror, of the forward cast. It incorporates the same principles of smooth acceleration and abrupt stop to propel the line. Make sure the rod stops with the tip at a high-enough angle to maximize the momentum of the line. A common mistake when using the backcast to deliver the fly is for the rod to drop toward the water's surface at the completion of the cast. This creates a large arc and destroys the mechanics of the cast. Also, keep an eye on the target during the delivery. When using the backcast I prefer to open up my stance so that a visual of the target can be gained with only a slight turn of the head.

Casting the large wind-resistant flies required for musky fishing exposes any deficiencies in your casting style. Focus on a smooth acceleration on the back and forward cast and always use the double haul to increase line speed. And adjust the length of the cast for the conditions.

Solid casting skills are so important in musky fishing. With the quality of equipment and lines available today, there is little excuse for not having the tools to make you a good fly caster. But the key is good form and practice. Musky casting skills can be practiced almost anywhere, including your backyard or a park. Hone your skills before the season starts.

5 MUSKY HABITAT

Musky habitat is wide and varied. It wasn't until venturing out of my home waters that I began to realize the diversity of where *Esox masquinongy* calls home. Small creeks to the continent's largest lakes and rivers and everything in between can host musky populations. Some water can be intimidating from a fly-fishing standpoint—especially large, open expanses. Covering open water places fly fishing at a disadvantage when compared to conventional gear. However, one thing fly fishing has taught me is to be a student of the water that you fish.

A mouthful of fly. BRIAN PORTER PHOTO

Read the obvious visible signs on the surface, and try to piece together what is occurring underneath. This basic principle is extremely important in musky fly fishing. Understanding the type of water that attracts and holds musky at various times of the year is essential to maximizing the effectiveness of each and every cast.

This chapter will take an in-depth look at musky habitat and structure—what to look for and what to avoid. It will analyze how key structural items vary by type of water or by geographic location. As a fly fisher you must be able to identify obstacles and turn challenges into strengths. Becoming intimately familiar with a piece of water will go a long way toward understanding the key elements to success and working through the challenges it presents.

While musky structure is wide and varied, some common threads connect most musky holding water. As top predators, ambush is the musky's game. When positioned to feed, muskies will commonly be found near some type of transition. It can be a transition in bottom contour, breaks in aquatic vegetation, or where water of various currents meet. Bait will often use these same transitions for feeding or as travel lanes, providing the musky with the perfect spots to lie in wait. Sometimes musky structure will be subtle, and can be simply provided by large rocks and boulders in deep, placid pools. And sometimes musky water will be found by accident, as a hookup or follow in an unsuspecting spot might determine water that produces future activity for reasons not easily explained.

While nomadic musky in search of pods of bait may be found on big, open waters, structure is normally the key to locating fish. In fact, mature musky often occupy the best structure based on their stature in the food chain. Searching out the best structure on any body of water can provide the key, eliminating less-productive spots and focusing on areas that are most likely to draw and hold mature fish.

Musky Water

Musky have proven to be adaptable to almost any type of water. This includes still water lakes and impoundments as well as flowing creeks and rivers, some with significant current flows.

The key to approaching any body of water that holds musky is not being intimidated by its general character but instead focusing on the elements that can be recognized as potential holding structure. With a thoughtful approach successful patterns will often develop that will allow you to gain confidence and expand on your knowledge base.

Choosing the type of water to be fished will often be based on personal preference or proximity. But there is no need to be limited. Fly anglers can cover the largest of rivers and lakes nearly as effectively as small streams and rivers.

Lakes

Musky lakes range in size from a few hundred acres to being miles across. Lakes are probably the most intimidating type of water to approach with a fly rod. The sheer amount of surface water can be overwhelming, and breaking down the details of the structure can require a significant effort. In larger lakes muskies can be nomadic and not relate to specific structure, creating a nearly insurmountable challenge for a fly fisher. But even in the largest lakes, musky will readily be found near structural elements.

One of the advantages of lake fishing is the ability of anglers to spread out. On most lakes you can find sections of water removed from other anglers. And with the information resources available today, it has become much easier to gain knowledge on how to approach a lake. One of the disadvantages of lake fishing is that specialized equipment can be required. Bigger boats with electronic gear are the key to covering large areas of surface water. While the wind can be used to push the boat in order to cover water, an electric motor will be helpful when trying to stay close to specific structure.

Finding likely holding water in lakes can be easier than it seems. Paper or downloadable maps as well as satellite imagery can help identify such structural elements as points, bays, dramatic changes in bottom contour, weed beds, and weedy edges. On some lakes most of this structure will be found close to the shore, but significant weed beds or reefs can also be found in the main body of the lake. I generally attempt to find water that is 20 feet in depth or less. Ten to 12 feet or less of depth maximizes the time that the fly stays in a zone where it is most likely to show itself to a musky.

When fishing lakes the focus should be on ambush holding areas created by the shoreline jutting into the

Lakes of various sizes host musky populations throughout its range.

lake, islands, dramatic changes in bottom contour, water temperature, and weed beds. All these structural elements will be discussed in detail later in the chapter. While lakes can be intimidating, fly-fishing techniques that provide a different look to the fish can be quite effective once good holding water has been identified.

Large Rivers

Large rivers from a few hundred feet wide to more than a thousand feet across present challenges similar to large lakes in terms of surface water. However, rivers usually have more visible structural elements such as islands, reefs, and soft, shallow inside bends, making it easier to identify potential holding areas when compared to a typical lake. Weeds in the softer areas also provide prime ambush areas in rivers, especially when located within easy access to deeper water.

The current of the river probably represents the biggest difference from fishing a lake. Current provides a means for moving a watercraft through or near potential holding water without the need for wind or an electric motor. However, oars or an electric motor may be required for positioning during the drift. As with a large lake, boats with motors powerful enough to move against the current allow for the best coverage of large river water.

The movement caused by the current requires some calculation, as casting targets will be moving by unless the speed of the drift is controlled or the watercraft is anchored. When drifting along, it is important to focus on your current cast and retrieve, but also to anticipate one step ahead.

One of the most challenging factors when fishing a large river is the wind. Maintaining a desired drift line can be difficult in windy conditions, even with the help of an electric motor. The wind will also make long, full casts difficult. The key to battling the wind on large rivers is to find the lee side of a shoreline or island. While positioning might not eliminate the wind, it can make the experience more tolerable.

Smaller Rivers

Large creeks and small to medium-size rivers from a hundred to a few hundred feet wide represent the most

Large rivers hold both opportunities and challenges for the fly angler.

inviting water for musky fly fishing. Holding structure is fairly easy to identify when compared to lakes and big rivers. Most smaller rivers can be covered with simpler watercraft such as drift boats, small pontoons, and even kayaks, making this an option for anglers without a boat. And since the structure will be mainly visible, there generally will be no need for sophisticated electronics to find holding water.

Most fly fishers will feel more at home on smaller rivers, since it is common to have had experience on this type of water for other species. They also give the overall sense of being more manageable. Casts will generally be shorter; and smaller rivers tend to be more protected from the wind, reducing the overall negative impact of breezy conditions.

Size of the river doesn't necessarily dictate the potential size of the musky. Big fish can be found in most smaller river systems. In fact, anywhere that is home to muskies with access to sufficient levels of protein in their diet, trophy-size fish are possible. Many smaller rivers are not large enough for motorized boats, even one with a jet motor, and are best covered by floating downriver from one point to another. Making a daylong commitment to the water is one of the most enjoyable ways to fish for musky, as this allows you to become immersed in the moment and focus on the task at hand.

A certain element of stealth is advantageous when fishing more intimate waters. Making casts without allowing the quarry to know of your presence will go a long way toward success on smaller rivers. This includes being quiet with and in the watercraft and not creating unnecessary disturbances on the water. Fly fishers have usually learned the value of a stealth approach.

Creeks

Even small creeks can harbor musky, as populations from larger rivers often extend into adjoining waters. The numbers found in some creeks may vary during the year and can be dependent on movements caused by spawning or feeding opportunities. However, musky densities on other creeks may stay more consistent throughout the year provided there is sufficient forage and cover.

Smaller rivers provide for a more intimate experience.

Some creeks are large enough for a canoe or kayak, while others are too tight or shallow for any type of watercraft. Smaller waters provide opportunity to anglers that do not have access to a watercraft, since most can be fished while wading or from the bank. Also, this type of water does not normally require the daylong commitment that is common when fishing bigger water or when floating a river.

While drifting from one point to another may be an option on some creeks, mapping out a handful of pools that can be hiked to is often the most efficient way to cover a musky creek. It can take some time to determine a few pools that either have good potential or are where a fish was actually encountered. Rotating these pools and working each thoroughly every outing will put you in position if a musky is ready to feed.

Big, slow pools and areas with timber or deadfalls are the most likely holding water on creeks. A stealthy approach will go a long way when fishing intimate waters. Focus on the best ways to approach the water with a minimum of commotion. Try casting from various angles, and work each level of the water column. Trees and brush along the creek can make casting a challenge. Get used to watching the backcast and fitting it into openings between trees or other vegetation. Roll or Spey casting techniques can be used in tight areas, but be careful to not create too much of a disturbance on the water's surface.

Structure

Elements of structure will be found in all the water types discussed above. Most muskies caught on a fly rod are not the result of a random act, and targeted casts to specific structure is the most effective way to increase the odds. Smaller fish species will use structure for both security and a feeding vantage point throughout their lives, but once a musky reaches a mature age and size, it will be at the top of the food chain and not necessarily need to use structure for security. While a musky may use structural elements to avoid the main current of a river or creek, structure will generally be used to ambush unsuspecting prey. When a musky is in an ambush position, it is likely to react positively to a well-presented fly.

The remainder of this chapter will focus on the various elements of structure commonly found in lakes,

Small streams can yield big results. Nate Carr with an impressive topwater musky. NATE CARR PHOTO

A visible weed bed in the early morning light. NICK PIONESSA PHOTO

rivers, and creeks. Analyzing and identifying structural elements is an important ingredient in successful musky fishing. Once identified, certain factors need to be considered before fishing. It is important to maximize the possibilities of each piece of structure every time it is covered. The position of the watercraft or angle of the cast in relation to the structure can impact the effectiveness of the presentation. While trial and error will always play a part, placing casts in the most likely spots given the type and level of structure will provide a consistent payoff. Let's take an in-depth look at musky holding structure.

Weed Beds

Weed bed is a generic term used to describe the sum total of a variety of aquatic plant life. Most are perennial plants that develop from the floor of the lake, river, or creek and can grow along the bottom or sprout up through the water column. Each species of plant has its own characteristics. Submerged plants have most of their mass below the water's surface. Various grasses, pondweed, naiad, water milfoil, fanwort, and broadleaf cabbage make up a good portion of submerged weed growth in North America. Most submerged plants have a fairly soft stem that prevents growth above the top of the water, though a few species will peek through the water's surface.

Emergent plants are generally rooted growth found close to shorelines. This type of plant will either cover the surface, as commonly seen with the pads of water lilies, or grow protruding through the surface, as seen with plants such as bulrush and cattails. Submerged plants will generally provide the best holding structure for musky. But since emergent plants often provide habitat for small fish and other aquatic life, they can be important musky hangouts on some lakes and rivers.

A weed bed creates its own functioning ecosystem. The plant life is host to microorganisms that feed small fish and other invertebrates. Weed beds also provide a place to live and feed for multiple species of fish of various sizes. Contained within a typical weed bed can be a slice of the entire food chain of that body of water. Such a vibrant and robust piece of structure is sure to catch the senses of the water's top predator. Weed beds also provide the

Steve Wascher works a fly over a sunken weed bed.

perfect background for a musky's natural camouflage. The coloration and general body markings of a musky allow it to fit almost seamlessly into the natural waterscape. This plays perfectly into the ambush style of its predatory ways.

Musky can be found in the main body of the weeds or within pockets in the weed beds, sitting motionless among the growth, ready to attack when given the opportunity. Presenting a fly over the top of the weed bed can be effective in raising a fish to the fly. With grasses and other plants that lie fairly flat, the fly may have to be fished down in the water column to effectively cover the weed bed. With plants that extend higher into the water column, casting over the top of the weeds may tempt fish that are suspended up toward the surface. This type of weed growth can provide the perfect opportunity for a surface fly.

Expansive beds with solid weeds can be somewhat problematic for finding fish. One of the best ways to find a musky in a large weed bed is to locate holes or breaks in the weeds. The edges created by the structure break create the perfect hiding and ambush point. The most productive holding areas in large weed beds are located where a musky has access to open water. Casting near an opening or break and retrieving the fly through it can produce explosive takes.

In larger lakes it is common for musky to be suspended above a weed bed, searching for schools of bait traveling the upper edge. In clear water this gives the predator a wide search area and allows it to use its stalking skills and closing speed. Running a fly high with a fast retrieve over sunken weed beds can be very effective in the summer and early fall.

In situations where the weed bed is fairly sparse, it is possible to retrieve the fly right through the weed stalks in search of musky positioned farther down. Retrieving the fly with a hard strip will force it through the weed stalks. A weedless hook setup or a fly tied with the materials acting as a hook guard will enhance the fly's ability to be pulled through the weeds.

Locating and spotting weed beds can be a challenge in itself. It is a fairly simple process when the tips of the weeds push past the surface of the water. This is common in shallow bays, sloughs, and along shorelines of lakes and rivers. Submerged weed beds in water of less than 10 to 12 feet in overall depth can normally be discovered in the daylight hours using polarized sunglasses. Weed beds have a distinctively

Musky in the weeds—an aggressive fish that attacked the fly along weed structure. BRIAN PORTER PHOTO

different look than open water. The weeds commonly appear darker and can be seen from a considerable distance under the proper lighting. Sunlit conditions will make it easy to spot submerged weeds.

Electronics can be essential in finding deep weed beds or locating weeds in murky water. Even basic sonar will provide reliable images of sunken weed beds and a guide to the approximate depth of the weed tops. Stripping a musky fly over the top of a deep weed bed can work well, and if you know the approximate depth of the weed tops and sink rate of your fly line, a simple countdown between the cast and beginning of the retrieve should put the fly in the fish zone. Not all the weeds grow to the same height, so it is inevitable that the fly will come in contact with some. But making adjustments to the countdown or speed of the retrieve will help you keep the fly above the weed tops.

Weed beds tend to grow in the same areas each year. The knowledge gained in locating a weed bed one year can often be successfully used in the future to fish the same area. But the size and density of a weed bed does tend to vary from year to year depending on growing conditions. Seasonal changes in water depth, temperature, and available light penetrating the water's surface can all impact aquatic weed growth rates. Conditions can have a one-year impact of low or even no weed occurrence in areas that have supported significant growth in the past. However, this is a fairly rare situation.

The introduction of exotic plant species can have a detrimental impact on native plant growth. Stewards of some watersheds put significant resources into efforts to protect native plant growth. Some exotics grow uncontrollably and choke out historic weed beds while changing the overall complexion of the lake or river's structure.

In northern climates weed beds go through a full transition during the course of the year. Weeds begin to grow in the spring as water temperatures rise and available sunlight increases. Weed beds will generally be most dense from mid-spring to late summer or early fall. This seasonal transition has a significant impact on the importance of weed beds as holding structure.

As weed beds expand in the spring, each layer of the food chain is slowly attracted to the habitat that it creates. Muskies seem to transition as well while the weed growth occurs and search out the first emergent weeds. Locating early growth of weed beds in the

The visible weed edge shows up as a darker mass in the clear water.

spring and early summer is one of the best ways to find musky at this time of year. Weed beds represent prime structure from late spring through mid- to late fall on most musky waters. As weeds begin to dissipate in autumn, musky tend to follow food sources or find other forms of structure for the remainder of the fall and winter. With longer growing periods, weeds can persist longer in southern lakes and rivers than northern musky waters. The key is to follow the growth and focus on this type of structure during periods when the weeds are robust and capable of attracting and holding a cross section of the food chain.

Weed Edges

Weed edges represent the beginning point of a weed bed. While this type of structure can be considered an extension of the topic discussed above, the edge of a weed bed creates such an important holding and ambush area that it requires a specific discussion. The edge of a weed bed can be very distinct, with a sharp border between weed growth and open water. Other edges can be more tapered in appearance, with the start of the weed bed being defined by straggling weeds that increase in density.

In many ways, weed edges offer the ultimate ambush point. This is the exact line where bait and other sources of food enter and leave the heavier cover of the weed bed. Smaller predators moving into the weeds to find a meal become an easy target when exiting the bed into open water. And a musky positioned along the outside of the weed edge or just into the first layer of the weeds will be almost perfectly camouflaged with its body color and markings.

Any weed edge provides good musky structure, even those that are straight and fairly uniform, but variations in the weed edge create structural points that require special attention. Dips and cuts along a fairly straight edge provide a perfect spot to ambush unsuspecting prey traveling the weed edge. Cuts in the edge are most apparent in weeds that grow to or through the surface of the water, but changes in contour can also be determined by looking through the water's surface. The weed line can typically be determined by a variation in water color that will be pronounced in sunny conditions. Deep weed edges that can't easily be seen or followed by sight can normally be tracked with the use of electronics.

The ultimate type of weed edge structure is the inside corner. My fishing partner Steve Wascher taught me how productive corners can be. Years of bass fishing have taught Steve numerous lessons with respect to structure. Inside corners are created by an abrupt change in the direction of the weed edge. This can be caused by a contour change in the shoreline or where the weed edge itself changes course because of the makeup of the lake or river's floor. In either case the area around the angle in the weed edge caused by the change is high-percentage ambush water. The inside corner is a particularly important piece of structure on lakes and deserves extra attention on any musky water.

I also like weed edges that have a tapered edge that leads to open water. This type of edge seems to be best when there is also a change in depth. I have had numerous encounters on my home water by casting into 3 or 4 feet of water with a bottom of fairly solid sand grass and drawing the fly back into water of 8 to 10 feet over a broken weedy edge. This type of structure makes it easy for a musky to move to and from this potential feeding area.

Weed edges can be covered with various approaches. When the main body of the weeds is submerged, positioning your watercraft on top of the weed edge and retrieving the fly out of the deep water toward the edge has proven to be very effective on some lakes. Positioning the watercraft off the edge can also be effective and is the only approach for weeds that protrude through the surface. You can then cover the weed edge from a perpendicular position by casting to the weeds and retrieving back. You can also position the boat near the weed edge and draw the fly right along the edge in both directions. I put extra effort into covering an inside corner. Making casts at various angles to the corner increases the odds of presenting the fly in a manner that will trigger a response from a musky.

Timber and Brush

Downed trees and overhanging brush represent some of the best musky structure on rivers of all sizes. This type of structure is particularly important on rivers with a heavy concentration of deadfalls and logjams. On a few rivers I have fished, timber was the main structure that held musky. Timber provides a perfect ambush point, and various levels of the food chain will search out this type of cover. The general appearance of logs and downed trees allow a musky's elongated

Working some ideal-looking musky habitat formed by a logjam along the river's bank. NICK PIONESSA PHOTO

body to blend in with the surroundings. A musky can position itself along the outside of a logjam or tuck its body inside an opening in the logs to gain the ultimate ambush advantage.

Logjams are often found along eroded banks where exposed roots give way from the bank. Large logjams that collect other floating logs and trees during high-water events are commonly found in bends in the river and in other slower-current areas where the shoreline contour creates a point that accumulates logs and debris. You should make multiple casts to a logjam before floating past it—slow the boat down or even anchor up so that you can cover the wood thoroughly, and at different angles. If a musky is tucked into the logjam, its window of vision may be limited, so you may need to make multiple casts to elicit a response.

Wood and timber do not have to be in the form of a logjam to provide effective musky cover. Even single logs along the bank or in the middle of the river consistently hold musky. For logs in the main flow of the river, those that run parallel to the current will be most effective since a musky can lie facing into the current but have its body positioned right along the log. This provides very effective camouflage. Logs that lie on or near the bottom but have enough of an opening underneath for a musky to partially position itself are highly preferred.

I have been amazed at some of the fish that have been drawn away from single logs. I remember staring at a lone log in fairly shallow water and thinking that if a fish was home, it would have been easy to detect. Luckily I made a cast anyway, and a stout musky pounced on the fly as it swam along the log. It wasn't a huge fish, but it was a big lesson learned. When fishing to a single log, any cast that lands close will do. But if I have the proper angle, I like to retrieve the fly along the log. If a perpendicular cast is needed, it is best to position the fly toward the upstream end of the log, allowing it to swing as it is retrieved.

Brush that hangs down from the bank or is growing into the water also produces quality holding structure. Musky use branches and vines in a similar way as weed growth. Equally important are overhanging branches that do not reach the water's surface. Dense branches block out light and allow a musky to lurk dangerously in the shadows. A tight casting loop or a sidearm approach is typically required to place a fly under the overhang, but placing the fly deep into the structure, up along the bank, may be required to entice a crafty musky.

Soft Water

In sections of river that have a fast to moderate current flow, musky will commonly find softer water that is out of the main flow. Water with a light or even no current flow provides a musky with an efficient holding spot, using little energy while in wait for an ambush. Soft water located immediately next to the main flow can be particularly productive, as bait will move between the faster and slower currents to feed.

Soft flows are commonly the result of shoreline contours and islands. Points that protrude from the bank produce eddies and small bays off the main flow. These areas are often productive from a fly-fishing perspective because fish positioned here can be aggressive. The downriver side of an island also produces a similar type of soft water, especially where the depth changes from the shallow point of the island to deeper water. Rivers that break into braids can produce a series of soft-water holding areas below each small island. Eddies and downriver sides of islands have produced numerous encounters for me over the years.

Soft holding water is not always readily apparent. Subtle breaks where the main flow pulls away from the bank can also be productive. These spots are usually not as obvious, but keep an eye open for any water that appears still compared to the main flow, even if it is only a foot or two wide. If there is enough depth along the bank for a musky to feel secure, the soft water creates a respite from the current while positioning the fish in a potential ambush spot.

If there is one thing that my home river has taught me is that musky search out soft water. On big rivers the visible signs will be hidden, but breaks in the main current will be created by bends in the river and bottom contour. Any area where the current slows significantly has proven to hold musky.

On some waters, mid-river eddies created by large boulders or logs just below the surface can hold fish. On a recent rip to Wisconsin, I fished with North Woods musky expert Brad Bohen. He stressed the importance of placing a fly into every mid-river break in the current, even if it was fairly subtle. These eddies are known to hold aggressive fish that will quickly pounce on a fly if it happens into its holding area. Brad

Blane Chocklett retrieves a fly through soft water created by a protruding point in the river.

also pointed out that some of his largest muskies have come from mid-river eddies.

Reefs

Significant changes in bottom structure will attract aquatic life from the entire food chain. Shallow reefs where the bottom rises up from the depths to create a rocky shelf commonly host variously sized bait and gamefish using the bottom contour to their advantage for feeding purposes. It is common to find smallmouth bass using rocky reefs to corral bait and to find crayfish. Rocky reefs are important bottom structure on lakes as well as rivers, and reefs that provide access to deep, open water can produce large muskies.

Muskies in feeding mode will often be positioned near the edge or lip of the reef. This provides the perfect vantage point for bait traveling along the edge or for food sources moving to and from the top of the reef. A reef doesn't have to represent a dramatic depth change to provide an effective holding area.

Reef water can be approached from various angles. I have had consistent success covering this type of water by allowing the craft to drift into the shallower water with the push of the current or wind while working the fly at an angle to the structure. Allowing the craft to drift off the reef into deeper water can also be productive but may not allow the fly to get deep enough when covering a dramatic change in depth. Where current or wind push are not a factor, making casts that draw the fly parallel to the structure will provide the best coverage.

Drop-offs and Boulders

Depth changes do not have to be dramatic to hold both prey and predator. Drop-offs of just a foot or two in moving water will allow a fish to get out of the main current flow. In moving water, musky will sit in these divots along the bottom to conserve energy. A drop-off will generally represent basic holding structure to a musky more than it will ambush water.

Almost any bottom contour change is worth exploring when hunting muskies. In big, deep water situations, electronics can reveal subtle changes in the bottom, and GPS coordinates will assist in finding the same piece of structure in future outings. In moving water, bottom structure changes will often show as a

A musky that was hooked and landed near a shallow reef. NICK PIONESSA PHOTO

disturbance on the water's surface. This is even true in fairly deep water.

Boulders in moving, deep flows also provide the type of water that consistently attracts musky. Large boulders in deep water often create boils and swirling currents on the surface, and the topwater disturbance can be pronounced on placid pools. The areas behind, around, and even in front of a boulder create soft water and provide the perfect resting spot for a musky. While this type of water may not represent a prime ambush hold, a fish positioned mid-river near a deep boulder can be tempted into striking with the right cast. Most deep structure can be covered as the watercraft drifts nearby or over the prime spots. Anchoring the craft near structure that has a good chance of holding fish allows the water to be covered more thoroughly.

Boulder-strewn pools are good targets for anglers fishing without a watercraft, providing potential structure that can effectively be covered by a walk-and-wade approach. Boulder fields or rock formations created or deposited by the last ice age make for rapids or small falls on many shallow rivers. This type of structure can create soft pockets and pools while restricting the upstream movement of bait—a perfect feeding situation for a musky. Approaching these areas on foot can yield surprising results. Each pocket or pool may need to be worked thoroughly and from various angles in order to get a musky to move to the fly. Casting angles when covering this type of water by wading may be impacted by shoreline structure, requiring both forward and back casting to properly position the fly. This can also be a good situation for a switch rod so that a Spey cast can be made, all but eliminating the casting obstructions along the shoreline.

Deep-Water Pools

On rivers of all sizes, deep-water retreats will be a preferred holding area for musky. Every river that I have fished seems to possess a number of deep pools that provide consistent musky encounters. Deep-water pools are also prime areas to search for big fish that lurk in the depths. Even rivers of modest size may have pools that drop off to 10 to 20 feet or more. On big rivers the depths can even be greater. Because the current flow near the bottom of deep water will be minimized, a musky can hold in a deep-water pool while using very little energy.

Covering a deep water pool.

Deep pools with boulders, ledges, and other bottom contours hold the greatest potential. This structure not only provides resting water out of the main current, but also creates hiding spots for a predator. Since fish from all levels of the food chain can be located in deep, open water, a musky can easily find a morsel or a meal. Once a musky finds a deep pool that it is comfortable in, it may spend a good portion of its time within the confines of that water.

Musky in deep-water pools may not operate with the same hair-trigger attitude as a fish positioned along a log or weedy edge. Deep-water fish are often more relaxed and may take some extra coaxing to generate interest in the fly. A deliberate approach to fishing deep-water pools can be very effective. Fishing with guide and musky expert Blane Chocklett in Virginia showed me how effective a deliberate approach to deep pools can be. Once a deep-water pool has been located that has produced multiple encounters, Blane works the water with a calculated, methodical strategy. By anchoring in the current, you can cast multiple times from various angles and completely cover the water. After thoroughly covering a portion of the pool, lift the anchor and allow the boat to drift down to a new station. Here the anchor is dropped and this section of the pool is covered as thoroughly as the last. An aggressive figure eight movement at the end of each cast is aimed at enticing lazy followers into striking. And experience has dictated that some of a river's largest fish will be located in slow, deep-water pools.

Musky in deep-water drop-offs in lakes can behave similarly to those in deep river pools. In lakes musky will use the dark, deep water for security and to have access to the range of food there, including schools of bait that roam the open water. The best deep-water areas in lakes tend to be close to structural elements such as weed beds and significant drop-offs.

Sandy Bays and Bars

Some musky will use the sandy areas of shallow bays and bars for spawning in the spring. As the spawn concludes, fish often linger, as this shallow water warms faster than the surrounding deeper water. This is especially true of bays and bars with a southern exposure. Laid-up fish can be found in and around sandy shallows as the spring water temperatures rise toward summer levels.

We found this musky cruising a sandy bar. NICK PIONESSA PHOTO

Musky found in shallow flats early in the year provide a great opportunity for sight-fishing. This can greatly reduce the number of casts needed to catch a musky. Some musky will be found motionless in the shallows, while others cruise the flat in a slow, methodic fashion. But often the highest percentage of fish will be found along the edge of the flat as the water begins to deepen.

Either the push of the wind, an electric motor, or a push pole can be used to move the watercraft across a flat to search for fish. This approach is similar to hunting bonefish or tarpon on a saltwater flat. Sunny conditions provide the best visibility. It is important to have a high vantage point on a raised deck or a platform, as spotting a fish before it sees or feels the presence of the boat greatly increases the opportunity for success.

When fishing sandy flats in the spring and early summer, actively spawning musky may be present. Do not target or disturb spawners. When actively engaged in spawning, musky will pair up and typically move slowly across the flat. The female will lead, with the male right next to and slightly behind her. Sometimes more than one male will fight and maneuver for position next to the female.

Man-Made Structure

Do not overlook structure that has been put in place for water management, power generation, or other purposes. Break walls designed to protect natural shorelines or define harbor areas often collect concentrations of bait at various times of the year. Heavy winds blowing toward a break wall often cause the wave action to push bait up against the wall in a vulnerable position. Musky can easily cruise along or set up for an ambush close to the structure. Docks and pilings located along shore, especially during the transition to the summer range, can attract a musky looking to feed on bait or panfish found in the shallows at this time of year.

Dams and the resulting outflows from a reservoir can be musky magnets. The area below a dam often has a significant amount of fish activity. Fish of all sizes can be attracted to this area due to the food source produced by the operation of the dam. Bait drawn through the sluiceway or turbines will often be stunned or mutilated, creating an easy meal and attracting the food chain. Musky have the option of feeding on stunned bait or moving up the chain to take advantage of larger fish attracted by the feeding opportunity. The amount of

Searching for musky below a power dam.

bait found below the dam can vary during the year and is often impacted by bait migrations.

Musky can congregate below the outflows of a dam for the potential food supply.

The area just below a dam usually includes deep walls with right angles—perfect places for musky to wait in ambush. The prime area is the soft water located alongside the flow or current of the discharge from the dam. The soft pocket created along the dam structure just to the side of the main flow is the most likely place to find a musky. It may take numerous casts to get a fish interested in striking. Musky are attracted to the area below a dam in the winter, as a consistent food source is possible while expending very little energy. The water for a few miles below the outflow can also be productive, as stunned or damaged bait will often be found well below the dam.

Bait Migrations

On most waters, especially big rivers and lakes, migrations of bait can directly impact the areas where concentrations of musky will be found. This positioning factor can be most significant in the late summer and fall when musky generally focus on a high-protein diet. An understanding of the local fall migration patterns of schooling bait such as shiners and ciscoes can lead to great opportunities for trophy-size fish.

When bait is available, musky may not relate to a specific structural element. The movements and holding patterns of the bait can bc driven by temperature stratifications in the water column resulting in the bait being located away from obvious structure. Musky may remain close to the school for easy access to a meal when the mood strikes.

When searching out concentrations of bait, look for softer water when fishing rivers and streams. The water around creek mouths can provide significant differences in water temperature and attract large concentrations of bait in the spring and fall. Consider water stain a type of structure. Pockets of water that is a bit dirtier than the main body of water from runoff or wave action can act as a layer of protection for bait. Focus on the stain edge, as predators will cruise the transition from dirty to clear water in search of bait that either gets disoriented or is on the move. Musky can be quite aggressive if found in this situation.

Water Temperature

The impact of water temperature can be seen throughout the year on all musky water. Water temperatures combined with available daylight will determine the growth pattern of weed beds during the spring and summer and play a role in determining how long weed structure stays in place into the fall. Also, baitfish will search out their optimum seasonal water temperature. The result is that water temperature can have a profound impact on the development of productive areas on your favorite musky waters from year to year. I have experienced a number of seasons where the most productive areas on a river or lake one year were not nearly as productive in successive years. The one factor that seemed to have the greatest impact was how structure and bait migrations were impacted by the changes in seasonal water temperature patterns.

Musky can be caught in a range of water temperatures from the 30s to 70s. Within that range I prefer fairly stable water temperatures. However, a steady increase in temperatures in the spring and summer or steady decrease in the late summer and early fall can trigger greater musky feeding activity. Rapid decreases in water temperature caused by extreme cold fronts normally have a significant negative impact on musky behavior and from an angling standpoint are best avoided if possible.

Water temperatures below the mid to low 40s will lower a musky's metabolism and activity. At the low end of the water temperature spectrum, I work the fly much slower than during the remainder of the year. Water temperatures in the 70 range speeds up the metabolism of a musky causing it to eat more often. But be careful—water temperatures in the height of the summer can rise to a point of being dangerous for musky survival after a spirited fight. The combination of low dissolved oxygen levels with the overexertion of a fight can be lethal.

I hooked this musky in front of a creek mouth that empties into the main river. NICK PIONESSA PHOTO

6 PRESENTING THE FLY

Success in fly fishing often comes down to proper presentation of the fly. Placing the fly at the proper depth and imparting the right retrieve directly impacts the amount of attention a musky will give to your offering. The casting and retrieve angle with relation to the targeted structure also plays an important role in enticing a musky. Subtle adjustments or differences in presentation and approach can have a significant impact on the entire process.

Retrieving the fly through prime musky water.

Many encounters with a musky will be visual and close to the boat. Being able to turn an encounter into an eat will dramatically increase overall success rate during a season. Multiple strategies are used for close-in work with a musky. Most musky guides would agree that the last 10 to 20 feet of the retrieve are the most important. This chapter will look in depth at the art and science of working the fly at the end of the retrieve and extending the time it is in the water. Every close encounter is different, but reacting quickly to the situation is the key. When an angler uses the fly rod with precision and purpose, a musky can often be taunted, teased, and soothed into taking just inches from the boat.

Once a musky eats, there is still a long way to go before the fish is brought to hand. A successful landing begins with meeting every take with a firm hook set, but the fight itself gets tense when a big fish has been brought near the boat. Many fish are lost at this point. Remaining calm and in control while having a solid plan for landing the fish will go a long way toward ultimately landing a trophy.

This chapter will look at various techniques for presenting a fly and for enticing, hooking, and landing a musky. It needs to be a full-on approach that is applied consistently and with purpose. Successful musky fishing is built on a certain element of repetition. Applying good techniques and habits every time on the water develops the foundation for always being prepared. And since you never know when the next take is going to occur, being always at the ready will pay off over time.

Retrieves

The basic one-hand retrieve is made by drawing in line with the line hand while pinching the line against the rod handle with the index and middle finger of the rod hand. Maintaining constant control of the line relies on having the line always pinched off against the cork for the entire time between completing the cast and beginning the next one. This allows you to keep a tight line and be in position to set the hook at any time the fly is in the water.

The line is then stripped by grasping it with the index finger and thumb of the line hand just behind where the line is pinched against the cork and moving the line hand with a down and rearward motion. The movement of the line hand then has a direct impact of the movement of the fly in the water. Some anglers use a stripping glove that both protects the fingers from line burns and provides extra grip so that line won't slip through the fingers when retrieving the fly or setting a hook.

During the basic retrieve I place the rod tip in the water to assist with depth control and reduce slack in the line. The tip in the water also provides for a stealthier approach, since line isn't ripped from the surface during the retrieve. But more importantly the tip in the water positions the rod for the proper hook set.

Speed, cadence, and motion of the fly can all be controlled. The movement of the line hand can create variations in presentation to meet certain water conditions or match the general mood of the fish, and one type of retrieve will often work better than another on a specific piece of water. But no matter what, it is important to realize that there is more than one way to retrieve the fly, and it can be a mistake to be locked into only one approach.

Let's first look at retrieve speed. A rapid and continuous movement of the line hand will result in a fast retrieve. It takes some practice to be able to quickly and repeatedly grab the line just below the rod hand to consistently maintain the speed of the fly throughout the entire retrieve. A fast-swimming fly can act as a trigger mechanism to a musky, since a quickly fleeing meal often causes a fish to make a snap decision, resulting in a take. This approach can work on an aggressive fish lying in wait or for a lethargic musky that needs the prodding of extra stimuli.

Speed has long been used by gear fishermen as a presentation factor. High-speed trolling on some waters has historically been productive, and reels with high-retrieve ratios allow gear anglers to crank their lures at an extremely high rate. It is difficult or impossible to replicate this type of speed with the standard retrieve. When going for maximum retrieve speed, some fly anglers opt for a hand-over-hand approach. While this may not increase the speed of the fly while it is stripped, it eliminates the pause between the strips of the basic retrieve method and provides an overall faster movement between two points.

The hand-over-hand method is accomplished by placing the reel and butt of the rod under the arm of your dominant side. The rod is then held in place by

Completing the one-hand retrieve by extending the line hand down and back.

pinching it between your arm and body. Positioning the reel so that it is located just behind the arm helps to secure the rod. Now both hands are free to strip line. The retrieve is made by alternating use of both hands to maintain a continuous movement of the fly. One hand grabs the line just behind the stripping guide and pulls the line until it is even with the body. Before letting go of the line with that hand, the opposite hand then grabs the line just behind the stripping guide. The process is then repeated until the fly is completely retrieved. The two-handed strip works best by rotating the body so that the foot of your non-dominant side is placed forward. The rod should be held so that the tip is in the water. With the foot of your dominant side back, the body is turned to give your hands a free range of motion to make long, fast strips.

If a fish takes the fly while using the two-handed-strip approach, the hook is set with a sharp strip-set using the hand that is closer to the stripping guide. The two-handed approach is a good option for adding more speed to the fly and can be a productive change of pace when other retrieves aren't working. This approach takes some time to become comfortable with, and it is a bit more cumbersome for setting up a figure eight at the end of the retrieve.

The need for speed can be linked to water temperature. Late spring, summer, and early fall water temperatures will usually have a musky's metabolism on high, and a fast retrieve will likely be effective. As water temperatures drop through the 40s and into the 30s, musky activity slows dramatically. In late fall on northern rivers, I have found a slow, deliberate retrieve to be more effective than a speedier approach. When the water temperatures drop, I prefer to work the fly deep with a slow strip-and-pause presentation. Takes of the fly will commonly be subtle in colder water conditions.

When using the basic one-hand retrieve, the cadence of the stripping motion can be as important as speed. The cadence is the amount of pause between each strip. A short pause gives the fly more of a continuous motion, while a longer pause between each strip gives the fly a more stop-and-go look in the water. Each

The two-hand retrieve provides an option for adding more speed to the fly.

Bill Dawson fooled this musky with an erratic stripping motion.

approach seems to work at times. The pause gives the fly the appearance of being injured and more susceptible to a predator.

The cadence can also be used to control the depth of the fly. A longer pause between strips will swim a sinking-tip or weighted fly at a greater depth, since the pause in motion allows the tip and fly to sink between strips. A shorter pause has the opposite effect and keeps the fly riding higher in the water column. A fast strip with a short pause can be used when fishing water that is shallow when compared to the sink rate of your sinking-tip. This will keep the fly off the bottom.

One other key element of the standard one-hand strip can be used for variation. The motion of each individual strip of the fly can either be smooth and consistent or accelerated and erratic, or something in between. A more consistent strip gives the fly an even and level movement in the water. I prefer a smooth retrieve when fishing cold water, as this gives the appearance of bait that is lethargic due to the water temperature and makes the fly easily accessible to a musky with a lowered metabolism.

A very quick and accelerated strip creates the opposite effect, making the fly jump or dart in the water. This quick movement can catch the eye of a nearby musky. A quick, accelerated strip combined with a pause of a few seconds gives the fly the appearance of bait that has been injured or is in distress. This approach is effective for getting a musky to commit to a take. I like to make the stripping motion with acceleration and an extra snap at the end.

Imparting the extra snap doesn't just make the fly dart forward, but will also move it from side to side. This adds another dimension to the motion of the fly and presents it at various angles, which seems to provide a trigger mechanism for a musky that is interested in or following the fly. While the reaction of each individual fish varies dramatically, there does seem to be a correlation between the fly changing direction and a musky attacking the fly. Flies that have good movement in the tail section will accentuate the directional change. This erratic strip approach was first shown to me by Ontario guide Ken Collins and has led directly to success on some waters.

When using the erratic strip-and-pause approach, a take will often occur during the pause. The enticing movement of the fly darting to the side and then pausing in a vulnerable manner can induce a musky

Nick Pionessa retrieves the fly with proper rod position, which includes placing the tip of the rod in the water.

to attack. When a musky takes during the pause, there will be weight at the end of the line as the next strip begins. This can work in your favor, as the next hard, erratic strip can result in a solid hook set—a significant advantage of this style of retrieve. Some of the most effective fly designs are created to accentuate a side-to-side erratic motion.

Some fly designs can attain this erratic action with just a basic smooth retrieve. Experienced musky angler Joe Goodspeed has developed a series of flies using Goop to shape and cover the heads. The shapes range from a bulbous head to a flat design. The round-head fly moves from side to side with a basic retrieve. The flat head creates a complete erratic presentation, giving the fly the appearance of being stunned, dying, and in peril. This action has proved to be effective in clear water and on fish that receive regular fishing pressure, and also provides a change of pace that may trigger a wary fish into taking.

The erratic strip with pause doesn't match up for all types of structure. It works best in open water when working over weed beds or in big, deep pools. Making a long pause isn't as practical when working tight, specific structure while floating a river. Covering structure like fallen timber or small eddies requires a cadence that keeps the fly swimming through the structure at the proper angle.

When stripping the fly, rod angle is important. Placing the rod tip in the water during the retrieve has a number of advantages. I place the first few feet of the tip down in the water during the retrieve. With the rod tip below the surface, the line remains quiet as it is retrieved, providing increased stealth. Also, maintaining the rod tip in the water keeps the fly swimming deeper in the water column all the way to the boat. This makes it more likely for a musky that is following the fly to stay interested throughout the retrieve and engage in a figure eight at the end of it.

The rod tip in the water approach also seems to result in more solid hookups. This angle forces you to use a strip-set when a fish takes, and the tip in the water causes the line to the fly to remain tight. This combination of factors leads to consistently deeper hook sets and makes it less likely to pull the fly away from a fish that just nips or pulls at it. Keeping the fly moving until there is a solid take prevents the fish from losing interest in the fly. With the rod tip above the surface of the water, the tendency is to set the hook and pull the fly away from an interested musky.

The only disadvantage of the tip below the water is that you lose the ability to use it to add action to the fly. Moving the rod from side to side in combination with a sharp stripping motion will accentuate the movement of the fly. The resulting erratic swimming pattern gives the fish a side view of the fly, which can be a triggering factor for a take. Also, a tip above the water's surface can assist in adding action to a topwater fly.

Presentation

Depth

Good presentation involves showing a fly to a fish or prospective holding water in a way that is most likely to elicit a take. Presentation includes placing the fly at the right depth and proper angle to the structure. A variety of controllable factors play into good presentation. I am a firm believer that presentation of the fly is the most import element of success in fly fishing, and musky fishing is no exception.

Presenting the fly at the proper depth relies on getting the fly down and then maintaining the depth through the retrieve. The sink rate of the line is responsible for taking the fly down the desired distance. Lines with a sink rate of 8 to 9 inches per second are the most versatile when fishing water of depths of 8 to 10 feet and greater.

The depth of the fly can be controlled by allowing the tip to sink before beginning the retrieve. When fishing still or slow-moving water, or when fishing from a boat that is anchored, the line can be allowed to sink for a significant amount of time before beginning the retrieve. A rough calculation using the sink rate of the tip and the number of seconds allowed to sink will provide an estimation of the initial depth of the fly.

The countdown should only be considered a general guide. Factors such as the hydraulics of moving water or the buoyancy of a fly can result in a slower sink rate. When anchored in water with a moderate current flow, the tension on the line can prevent the tip from sinking at a normal rate. By angling the cast upstream and making a series of upstream mends, the tip is allowed to sink freely before the retrieve begins, thus maximizing the depth.

Some shooting-head-type sinking-tips are available with an intermediate running line, allowing the tip to get deeper and stay there longer than a floating running line. Sticking the rod in the water with the tip pointing down after the cast is completed will help the sinking-tip and line reach its deepest point. A weighted fly can also be a factor in depth control. The weight added through dumbbell eyes or other means allows the fly to sink at the same rate or even faster than the tip. However, a weighted fly is a bit more difficult to cast than an unweighted one. The retrieve and rod tip positioning will also have a direct impact on maintaining fly depth, as discussed earlier in the chapter.

Gaining maximum depth can be important when fishing big, open waters in a lake or river. Musky will readily move up to a fly, so scraping the bottom is not

On big water, attaining the proper depth can be the key to success.

Working a shallow weed bed with a topwater fly.

necessary. It seems that getting the fly down at least half the depth of the water puts the fly in the game. When fishing smaller rivers or areas of shallow structure on bigger waters, the fly may only need to ride down in the water column 2 to 3 feet. A tip with a sink rate of 3 to 6 inches per second or even an intermediate line may take the fly to its desired depth. A tip with a faster sink rate can still be used to cover shallow water. A faster retrieve and higher rod tip angle will allow the fly to ride up in the water column.

Sometimes placing the fly below the surface is not required at all. Topwater flies can bring musky to the surface in the right type of water under the proper conditions. Water depths of 8 feet or less in lakes or slower flows in rivers are the best areas to target with a surface fly. Open structure such as weed beds or eddies can provide the type of water where muskies will move to the surface. This type of structure also represents areas where muskies may suspend in the water column, placing their position closer to the surface.

For surface presentations, flies that push and move water will do the best job at gaining a musky's attention. Patterns that incorporate spun deer hair, foam, or wood heads allow the fly to remain on the surface and create a disturbance as it is retrieved. Surface fishing represents the ultimate in fly fishing for any species, and it is a special challenge when involving a potentially big fish like a musky.

When working a surface fly, the retrieve can be key to enticing a fish to eat. An abrupt, fast strip has the effect of pushing a lot of water and creating a commotion on the surface. This type of strip followed by a significant pause gives the impression of something injured and vulnerable. As an alternative, a surface fly that moves with a very short cadence between strips will appear as an object trying to flee the scene, which may trigger a musky to move to the surface. The take of a topwater fly by a musky can be explosive, but don't react too quickly and be sure to feel the weight of the fish after the visual take before setting the hook.

Fly Placement

Placement of the fly in relation to a structure or a suspected musky holding area can be the most important ingredient of good presentation. Allowing the fly to be accessible to potential musky holding water and fishing it through productive areas for

Teamwork can be critical. Mike Schultz hoists a hog that he landed on a trip to Wisconsin. MIKE SCHULTZ PHOTO

as long as possible will certainly add up to more encounters. Casting accuracy and distance will both play into proper fly placement depending on the water and structure type.

Casts should never be made without purpose. For each type of structure that is covered, I attempt to visualize where a musky will most likely be positioned before placing the fly in the water. The preferred presentation will be a fly that shows itself a few feet in front of and slightly above a musky's holding position. Making the right cast takes some planning and anticipation. Fly placement in water with a moderate current requires a different mental and physical approach than fishing slow pools in rivers or open water in lakes. Things happen faster when floating a river, and making the right cast at the right time becomes very important.

When floating a river, good holding structure can be fairly continuous. Quickly processing how to make the next cast while finishing the prior cast and retrieve is a skill that comes with experience, but is extremely important in terms of effective water coverage. A friend or guide controlling the boat can provide another set of eyes. Good communication between the angler and the oarsman is critical.

It is important that each cast covers as much structure as possible. This involves calculating the current speed to place the cast far enough upstream. Casts need to be accurate but not necessarily precise. Provided the water has sufficient clarity, a musky will move a distance to attack a fly, and dropping the fly in a reasonable vicinity should be all that is needed. Once a spot has been covered with a good cast, the next cast should be made to another spot or at a different angle.

Most of the time when floating, I prefer to get the fly moving almost immediately after it hits the water. The only exception is when casting into deeper water, where allowing a short countdown gives the fly a better chance of getting into a deeper zone. Moving the fly immediately combines the noise and disturbance of it hitting the water with instant movement, creating the perfect triggering mechanism. The immediate movement of the fly relies on not losing contact with the line as it shoots through the guides of the rod. Forming an additional "guide" with the thumb and forefinger allows you to handle the line and begin the retrieve as soon as the fly hits the water.

The amount of structure covered with each retrieve is maximized by the proper casting angle. Most of the time this is a crosscurrent angle to the bank or structure. But other times an area can be best covered by delivering a cast upstream to cover an eddy created by a bar or log pointing downriver. A downriver angle might be best to cover a downed log lying parallel to the current by allowing the fly to slowly sweep and swing the length of the log. Casting angle is also important when fishing along weed beds. When the weeds are deep enough, casting across and working any possible holes or crevices in the bed can be very productive. But changing the angle to cast upstream or downstream so that the fly is presented along the weed edge will allow the fly to cover the high-percentage holding area where open water meets the weed bed.

Retrieve speed can also control how thoroughly a piece of structure is covered. Slowing the retrieve down at specific times allows the fly to work the contour of structure such as a logjam or downed trees. However, adding speed at the precise time can prevent the fly from getting caught up in obstructions.

When covering slow-moving or still water, fly placement requires a different approach. Without the urgency to cover specific casting targets, the emphasis will be mainly on covering water through consistent casts that completely turn over the fly. Structural targets are now mainly submerged weeds, bottom contour changes, and boulders. The key is making casts at angles that cover the most water. Casting angles can be adjusted to present the fly to dark spots in the weeds or to cover a weed edge.

Working open water is more about presenting the fly in expansive areas and using a grid approach to ensure all the water is covered as opposed to casting to specific structure. When fishing open water, I focus on depth to make sure the fly is far enough in the water column to entice a musky's interest. But getting the fly deep is not as important if there is reason to believe that some fish may be suspended.

To effectively cover open water structure, the watercraft needs to move across its surface. The push of the wind, current, electric motor, or paddle can be used to move or reposition the watercraft. Using an electric motor requires focus to maintain a desired path while casting and retrieving. However, modern technology has resulted in electric motors that can be programmed to move along a predetermined course.

When fishing water with current, I use the electric motor to keep the boat pointed either directly into the

Eric Grajewski fights a fish in the waning light. Controlling the drift speed was a contributing factor to this hookup.

current or directly downriver. This allows for a cast and retrieve perpendicular to the current. When drifting with the wind in open water, I attempt to point the bow of the boat downwind. Casts can then be made out of each side of the boat in a perpendicular fashion to maximize water coverage. This also places the boat at an angle where casts will be made with a side wind as opposed to casting directly into the wind. But care needs to be taken when the wind is pushing onto your casting shoulder. Casts made downwind usually result in a less effective presentation, as the craft will be drifting toward the fly, resulting in difficulty in maintaining a tight line.

In heavy wind conditions, the boat may be pushed so fast that drift speed doesn't allow the fly to fish deep enough or cover specific structure. Pointing the bow of the boat downwind and controlling the drift speed by using a trolling motor in reverse is one approach to drift control. However, the most effective way to slow the drift is by using a drift sock, which acts like a parachute. Attached to the boat, it sinks underwater and the surface area of the sock holds the boat against the drift and slows down its speed. A drift sock can allow you to fish in windy conditions that may be otherwise unfishable.

I experienced this approach when fishing with musky fly angler and guide Eric Grajewski. He uses a drift sock combined with the electric motor if needed to maintain a drift speed of less than 1 mile per hour. Actually, 0.7 mile per hour is his target. At this speed the water can be covered methodically with a cast that remains relatively perpendicular to the boat. At a higher drift speed, the fly tends to swing to the rear of the boat. This forces the fly to lose its depth, and for the angler fishing in the bow, the end of the retrieve will bring the fly alongside the entire boat, which may reduce the opportunity for a boat-side take.

When fishing big, open pools in the slow-moving current of a river, anchoring and making a number of

I was able to spot this fish cruising in the shallows. NICK PIONESSA PHOTO

casts from one position can be extremely effective. Once the water has been covered from that anchor point, the boat is allowed to slip down the current and is anchored again to repeat the process. When anchored in one position, the key is to make each cast slightly different by varying the angle and countdown. A cast with a slight upstream angle followed by an upstream mend will allow the fly to attain its greatest depth. When anchored in the current, the fly will derive its swimming action by the retrieve as well as the swing created by the current's push on the fly line. The swing effect can be a triggering mechanism for a musky, as it gives the appearance of bait attempting to flee the scene.

When covering musky water, most casts will be made blindly to likely holding areas or ambush points, but occasionally the opportunity will arise to sight-fish for musky when the conditions are right. This normally occurs in the late spring or early summer as post-spawn fish transition to summer holds, seeking out the warming waters of sandy flats and bays with a southern exposure. Sunny skies and clear water enhance your ability to spot a musky in the water.

When a cruising or laid-up musky is spotted, I try to quickly assess the situation by identifying which way it is facing and whether it is moving. Try to look out as far as possible, as seeing the fish before it feels your presence is extremely important. A high vantage point will provide a farther sight line. If the angle of the boat allows, I attempt to make a cast well out in front of the fish, retrieving the fly across its sight line. I generally lead the fish by 10 feet or more depending on clarity. Placing the fly too close to the fish seems to create an unnatural situation and is less likely to trigger a strike. By placing the fly farther away, it is more likely that the musky will go into stalk and attack mode. If the musky is on the move, be sure to provide plenty of lead so that the fly stays well out in front of the predator.

Casting the fly at other than a right angle can also be productive. If the fish is laid up, a few different casting angles can be tried. But no matter what angle you use, keeping the fly farther from the musky rather than too close increases the chance of a predatory response.

Dealing with Follows

It can all at once be the most exciting and frustrating aspect of musky fly fishing when a big fish follows the retrieve all the way to the boat only to have it lose interest or run out of room before it eats the fly. But reacting to a follow is consistently the most visual part of musky fishing. It causes you to always be alert and focused as the fly approaches the boat. A high percentage of fish are hooked in the first 10 feet of the retrieve or the last 10. How you handle the up-close encounters can often define the success of your day or even an entire season.

Why exactly a musky follows a fly or lure to the boat has long been open to debate. It is a behavior that has been the focal point of many discussions while on the water or over a beer at the end of the day. Any apex predator has a certain swagger when roaming its environment, and following, circling, and generally terrorizing its potential prey all seems to be in the realm of top-of-the-food-chain behavior. One of the theories that makes sense regarding a musky following its potential prey involves attack angle. Blane Chocklett presented this idea to me after a lengthy discussion of musky behavior. The theory suggests that a musky prefers to attack from the side so it can use its teeth to grab its prey in the middle and use its powerful jaw to crush and kill. This allows the musky to then swallow its meal head first and limit the difficulties caused by sharp dorsal fins.

While I have witnessed the side-angle feeding approach in practice, I have also seen many musky take a fly directly from behind, which suggests that the issue of following the fly is more complex than simple attack angle. Each fish is an individual that has its own tendencies and mood swings based on such factors as water temperature, moon phase, barometer, how recently it last fed, and even water type. It seems that many factors are at play when it comes to whether a musky is ready to feed or simply shopping around. The apex predator factor means a mature musky has no need to act in an urgent manner. It then becomes the challenge to find a trigger point that causes a musky to eat the fly.

I have experienced plenty of musky takes while the fly is paused between strips, and in the early summer have even witnessed a number of fish eating the fly as it was stopped during a slow retrieve. Some followers can be coaxed into taking by pausing the fly as

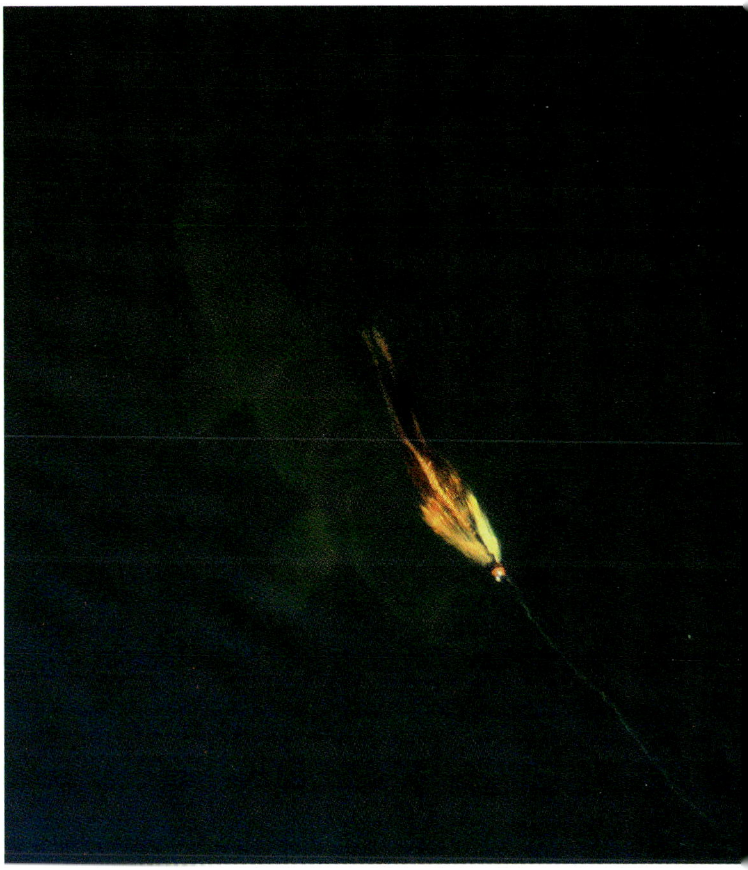

A big musky lurks behind the fly—one of the most exciting aspects of the sport. BRIAN PORTER PHOTO

it approaches the boat and slowly adding an enticing twitch. However, it has been my experience that most musky will lose interest in the fly if some speed or a change of angle is not added. I try to read the fish, and if it appears ready to pounce and in a mood where it might feed on a slow stop-and-twitch presentation, I will first give this a try. This approach may work best in colder water conditions.

Adding speed and angle change to the fly can be the best way to get a fish to eat at the side of the boat. This is where the figure eight technique becomes essential.

The figure eight is best initiated by speeding up the retrieve as the fly approaches the watercraft and then sweeping the rod with a movement of the arm either away from or across the body. This has the impact of changing the direction of the fly and allows you to easily roll right into the figure eight movement. The rod tip should remain in the water throughout the entire process. It seems that keeping the rod tip deep increases the chances of a take. The fly should also be drawn within a couple of feet or less of the tip to complete

This is the proper hand position for the figure eight—with the line pinched off by the rod hand and the line in the grip of the line hand to complete a strip set or gain control in case of a take close to the boat.

The figure eight is accomplished by extending the arms and keeping the rod tip deep while moving the rod across your body.

With arms extended across the body, make wide turns with the rod so that the musky can turn and follow while providing a side attack angle.

With the turn completed, bring the fly back in the opposite direction as the fly stays within two feet of the rod in order to make effective turns.

I use the figure eight after every cast whether I see a fish following or not. NICK PIONESSA PHOTO

the figure eight movement. I retrieve the fly to the knot between the main leader and bite tippet before beginning the figure eight movement. Using this knot as a guide provides a consistent stop point each time.

Using two hands on the figure eight allows for the power to move the rod through the water while keeping the tip and fly deep. The two-handed approach is best accomplished with a rod that has an extended butt and enough stiffness to move and turn the fly in the water. I keep my dominant hand on the main cork and my line hand on the butt section. I also grip the line with the line hand while performing the figure eight to maintain line control in case of a close-up take. The figure eight should be drawn by the rod with wide, arcing turns that will allow a musky, especially a large fish, to stay with the fly as it moves and turns. The wide arc also gives the fish a chance to see the fly from the side, providing an enticing attack angle. Extending the arms down and across the body before making the turn gives the figure eight its full range of movement, allowing a fish to continue to follow and be engaged with the fly.

If a fish continues to follow the fly into the figure eight, increasing its speed is the best trick for eliciting an eventual take. The speed factor can put the predator in attack mode and cause an instinctual response to prey in distress. It is important to continue to make wide arcing turns, especially when speeding up the fly, so that the musky doesn't lose track of the fly. Instead of drawing a figure eight, the fly can also be moved in a wide arcing oval. The theory behind using an oval is that it forces a wider turn, making the fly more accessible to the fish.

It is important to engage a musky in the figure eight as soon as possible. When a fish is following, the last couple strips should increase the fly's speed and then roll right into the figure eight. The key is to get the musky engaged in the pursuit of its prey to the point where its sole focus is on the fly. When a musky is "locked in," it seems to forget about its surrounding and not be fazed by being close to the boat or the rod sticking in the water.

Keeping the fly away from the boat during the figure eight does seem to increase the chances of having a musky stay engaged. Angling the rod tip out slightly during the figure eight movement is one step that places the fly away from the watercraft. Pushing the rod tip deeper during the figure eight also places the fly farther from the boat. I also try to make my first movement while rolling into the figure eight toward the bow when fishing in the front of the craft and toward the stern when fishing in the back. This places the fly away from the main surface area of the boat.

The figure eight should be employed every time, whether you see a musky following or not. Often a fish will follow but instead of trailing directly behind the fly, will remain low in the water column. A figure eight movement at the end of every retrieve can bring a lazy follower in for a close look or even a take. Be aggressive and consistent—two or three complete figure eights should be made at the end of every retrieve. Keep your eyes focused well below the fly and be ready for anything. If a fish follows or lingers below the fly, keep at it and speed up the fly until the fish eats or disappears.

Initially it may be hard to believe that the figure eight could be so effective—especially when there is no visible fish following the fly. But when you commit to performing the maneuver at the end of every retrieve, at some point you will become a believer. On some waters I estimate that aggressively using the figure eight at the end of every retrieve increases encounters and hookups by 50 percent. Finishing with a figure eight should be a standard move at the end of every retrieve.

Hooking and Landing

Getting a musky to take a fly is only half the battle. Hooking up and staying connected to the fish is another challenge in itself. Musky have tough mouths with as much exposed cartilage as meat. The entire roof of the mouth is nearly impenetrable by a hook, but there are enough sweet spots along the side of its mouth for the hook to make a solid connection. The key is in the hook set, which needs to be controlled and decisive.

The manner in which a musky eats a fly is not consistent. Sometimes it is a murderous attack aimed at

Strip-set and keep tight to the fish during the entire fight. NICK PIONESSA PHOTO

Try to stay positioned so that the pressure on the fish is up and from the rear. BRIAN PORTER PHOTO

swallowing the bait whole. This action is often completed by an accelerated take and a turn in the opposite direction. Other times the assault seems to be more of a mauling aimed at injury and capture. I have witnessed musky cruising with a mostly dead baitfish sideways in their mouth, and musky clamping down on the middle of a smallmouth hooked on a fly. Both of these behaviors indicate that musky chew and even kill their meal before eating. Still other times the grab is quite subtle, as the musky simply opens its large mouth while lunging forward and eating as it approaches from the rear. The subtle take from the rear may also occur with the musky simply grabbing the materials at the back of the fly and even behind the hook point, resulting in no chance for a hookup.

The manner in which a musky grabs the fly will have a clear impact on the hook set. Any take that involves a musky eating the full fly and turning away provides the best chance for a quality side-of-the-mouth hookup. Instances where the feeding motion is from the rear and the fish doesn't turn after eating the fly are certainly more problematic, as this angle exposes the hook point to more cartilage and lower-percentage hooking areas.

A solid hookup is best accomplished by setting the hook with a sharp strip-set. The direct movement of the line hand can pull the point of the hook deep into the mouth of the musky. Because leaders and tippets are generally constructed from strong materials, it is nearly impossible to set too hard. The strip-set has two distinct advantages over simply using the rod to set the hook. Aside from any stretch in the line, the strip-set creates a direct connection and eliminates the impact of the flex of the rod that can cushion the hook set. Also, the strip-set allows the fly to continue to swim if a musky eats but is not hooked, in which case the fish may continue to follow and try to eat the fly again. But a failed rod set usually pulls the fly too far away from the fish so that the chance of a follow or additional take is diminished or eliminated and the rod will not be in position to continue the retrieve of the fly.

Once a fish has been hooked using the strip-set, it is essential to engage the rod by placing a deep bow down to the cork. However, an effective strip-set may require continuation. A musky will often move in your direction after it eats the fly. The key is to keep stripping hard to maintain a tight line and to bury the hook as best as possible. I try to make sure that I have a tight connection to the fish before lifting the rod. Keeping the rod tip in the water seems to improve the effectiveness of the strip-set and makes it less likely to raise the rod too early.

When you are retrieving the fly and suddenly the line seems to go slack, this is most likely caused by a musky that has eaten the fly but continues to cruise or glide toward your position. The line needs to be stripped rapidly and without hesitation to get tight to the fish and to strip-set the hook point home. This decisive action could mean the difference between a solid hookup and the musky dropping the fly. Always be on guard for this sensation when retrieving the fly, which seems to occur more in open-water situations.

The strip-set may not be practical when working the fly in close to the watercraft or when using the figure eight, since there will be very little line beyond the rod tip and the rod can be positioned at an awkward angle when a musky takes the fly. In these instances using the rod to set the hook will likely be the only way to drive home the hook point. This can be risky, however, since setting too early can result in a handful of nothing. Be absolutely sure the musky has the fly before using a rod set. If using the figure eight, you should be able to see the take and feel the weight of the fish before setting the hook. The movement of the fly while using the figure eight will begin the hook set, and it can be completed with a sharp movement of the rod.

Once a musky has been solidly hooked, playing it by stripping the line is generally preferred over attempting to play the fish off the reel. Stripping the line is the best way to keep the line tight and maintain a deep bend in the rod. You should use any opportunity to take up line in order to keep a tight connection.

When a musky is hooked while close to the watercraft, it is best to allow the fish to move away when it is ready to run. Many fish are lost just after the hookup, as musky have a tendency to shake their head and throw the hook. Allowing the fish to run away from the boat has the effect of settling it down and continuing the fight on a longer line. The line must be allowed to slide through your fingers and the cork evenly and smoothly when the musky runs, but enough pressure needs to be applied to keep a tight connection to the

Things get exciting when a hooked musky is brought near the boat. BRIAN PORTER PHOTO

Eric Grajewski properly displays a good-looking musky for a couple of quick photos before its release.

fish. Make sure that loose line stays free to prevent it from tangling during the fight. A fishing partner can assist in keeping your line free of any obstructions.

Musky have a distinct fighting style. At times a battle with a musky seems more like a tug-of-war, with each side giving and taking until the fish tires. When a musky takes line, it will normally be in a long, steady pull or short, quick spurts of speed combining brawn with sprinter's speed. Occasionally a musky jumps with an explosive aerial display and should be met by bowing toward the fish. But mostly the fight will be below the water's surface, with the musky running through its repertoire of tricks to throw the hook. While a musky doesn't typically provide the sizzling runs and multiple jumps of other sought-after game species, a hookup with a musky is every bit as exhilarating, if not more so. The difficulty in hooking one fuels the excitement. There are few fish that can still make my knees knock during a fight like a big musky.

Despite your best efforts to place a fly firmly in a musky's mouth upon a take, certain factors such as the attack angle and whether the fish turns after taking the fly will affect the quality of the connection. A few steps can be taken to increase the odds, even if the hook position is tenuous. Keeping the line tight with a deep bend in the rod is a given. The preferred angle to fight a musky is to have the pressure applied from behind the fish, as this maintains a pull on the hook of back and up into the fish's mouth. I attempt to maintain this angle by the position of my arms and even by moving around in the boat. But when a musky makes a significant change in direction, little can be done in terms of adjustment. Unfortunately, many fish are lost when the angle of the fight takes a dramatic turn. When a fish is facing my direction, I will strip hard if it is moving toward me but may lighten up on the pressure if it is facing my way and simply holding, since too much pull from that angle can remove the hook from its mouth. When the fish is facing me, I try to apply pressure with a high rod angle so that the hook point is pulling up.

The end of the fight represents a high-risk period for losing a hooked fish. A musky will often throw the hook by quickly changing direction, violently shaking its head, or doing a series of rolls on or near the surface. Landing a fish will sometimes depend on how well it is hooked, but the chances of bringing a musky to hand will be increased by maintaining constant

Ready for the release.

deep pressure with the rod. As a musky shows signs that it is beginning to tire, bring it to the net or cradle as soon as possible. Musky are more sprinters than endurance runners and tend to tire rather quickly. Even a big fish can be landed in a fairly short period with sufficient pressure.

A musky cradle or a net is an essential tool for landing a fish and allows you to properly handle it for photography and release. The use of a cradle or net with soft, knotless catch-and-release netting is important so as not to damage the skin of the musky. A cradle allows you to keep the fish breathing in the water and lift it into the watercraft for a quick photo. The musky can then be placed back onto the cradle and lowered back into the water with limited trauma.

If using a net, in addition to soft netting it should have a large frame and deep bag. This allows the fish to sit freely and upright in the water at the side of the boat before a photo and release. For a photo, I prefer to lift the fish out of the net boat-side as opposed to lifting the entire net into the boat. Nets are more versatile than a cradle and are the only way to go when fishing alone. They are also much more effective landing tools, as most musky anglers have had at least one bad experience with a cradle, and for this reason I now use a net exclusively.

A few critical tools should be carried for quick, safe removal of the hook. Using barbless hooks will facilitate an easier removal. I carry a couple of pairs of heavy-duty pliers, one with an extra-long nose to reach deep into a musky's mouth if the fly has been devoured. I also carry spring-loaded jaw spreaders to open a musky's mouth when it is clamped shut or when the fly is deep. It is also recommended to carry bolt cutters in the event that a deeply buried hook can't be removed without causing injury to the fish. The hook can be cut at the bend. However, I would only use this approach in extreme cases.

For photographing a musky, everything should be ready to go before the fish is lifted from the water.

Grasping the fish firmly at the wrist of the tail with one hand and just behind the pectoral fins with the other provides reasonable control over the fish while holding it for a photo. This approach can be a bit more difficult with a larger fish, and it is critical to maintain a solid grasp of the wrist. Grabbing the fish by its jaw and supporting the rear of the fish just where the tail begins is another way to display a musky for a classic photo and gives you more control over the fish. With this approach the musky is less likely to get loose from your grasp and hurt itself by bouncing around on the floor of the boat. There is a fair amount of room just under the gill plate to firmly hold the jaw, but it is extremely important to not allow the hand to come in contact with the gills and cause serious damage to the fish.

I avoid using any tool that grabs the musky by the jaw. These tools can cause damage to the soft tissue of the lower jaw and even poke a hole through the tissue. I have seen evidence of damage caused by one such tool that later got infected, disfiguring the fish.

A musky should be lifted for a couple of quick photos and then quickly placed back into the water so it can breathe. Some additional shots of the fish can then be taken while it is in the water before its release. Prior to releasing a musky, I make sure that it is fully revived and strong before allowing it to swim away. By grasping the wrist of the tail and supporting the fish with the other hand behind the pectoral fins, the musky can be moved gently back and forth in the water. The fish should be facing the current when being revived in a river.

Before releasing the fish, I hold it using just my hand around the wrist to move the tail slowly from side to side in a swimming motion. I also tip the fish slightly to each side. At this point you should feel the fish making a swimming motion on its own. When the musky is ready to go, it will make a strong kick of the tail right out of your hand. I make sure that the fish is swimming properly as it moves from sight and lives to fight another day.

Brad Bohen did everything right to land this thick, late-fall, full-moon beast. BRAD BOHEN PHOTO

7 TALKING MUSKY WITH THE PROS

In recent years a number of serious musky fly anglers have emerged whose dedication have assisted in advancing the sport. Because individual encounters with musky are limited, the learning curve can be a long one if traveling the journey solo. This chapter contains a series of interviews with top anglers and professionals who passionately pursue musky on a fly. While musky anglers are generally reluctant to divulge information on their secret spots, they are more than willing to share their techniques, strategies, and insights. This chapter is aimed at giving the reader the opportunity to visit and learn from these top anglers.

Keep your hands away from those teeth. BRIAN PORTER PHOTO

Brad Bohen tying a musky meal along one of his beloved Wisconsin rivers.

BRAD BOHEN

LOCATION: WISCONSIN

Brad owns and operates Musky Country Outfitters in northern Wisconsin, specializing in guiding fly fishers to the diverse musky waters of the area. He was also featured in the fly-fishing film *Zero to Hero*, which explores the passion and zaniness of musky fly fishing. Brad is considered to be one of the pioneers and the top ambassador of musky fly fishing, and his work has helped popularize this form of the sport.

What attracted you to musky fishing with a fly?

For me, it was a merging of my passions. I fished for muskies growing up in Wisconsin with gear and bait from the time I was a boy. And then I had a parallel development in fly fishing—but that was all cold water. I went to school in Montana and loved trout fishing. I eventually found my way into streamer fishing for trout, and it occurred to me sometime in the '90s that I should try crossing these paths a little bit. It was an extension of my interests from different ends of the angling spectrum and bringing those together. There wasn't mush information available about musky fishing, so it was new and it was exciting. Plus we have this amazing warmwater resource right here in Wisconsin that people weren't really taking advantage of, so the attraction for me is it was something different that allowed me to expand what I already loved and doing it right in my backyard. And I took it from there.

What type of musky water do you prefer or regularly fish and why?

Everything—that is part of the attraction to me in my local fishing here in Wisconsin. We have everything from little feeder creeks to tiny natural lakes to sprawling man-made flowages, bigger natural lakes, and of course a variety of big, brawling rivers. I like to fish all of them. Seasonally it changes. At the beginning of the season, I may focus on areas that have concentrations of fish coming off the spawn. Then we go from there, setting up into the summer patterns. Later in the summer, the dog days match up really well with fishing top water in our cabbage-based clear-water lakes. And then come fall it's the larger rivers and systems where the big fish are found, so it gives us variety throughout the season.

I am blessed up here in Musky Country that we have a little of everything and we never get blowouts—because of the lakes, the flowages, and the different river systems, we always have fishable water. Most other musky fisheries are vulnerable to weather conditions. One thing about northern Wisconsin is that water pretty much flows down from here—we are in the headwaters. That is an ideal scenario for chasing these fish. What I really enjoy is the Canadian Shield–type water: clear, deep-water lakes with giant muskies and that doesn't see many anglers. While I don't have that in my backyard, I can get in a floatplane and be there in an hour.

What are the unique aspects of the water that you regularly fish?

In northern Wisconsin we have an incredible supply of naturally occurring musky. It can be debated that the natural distribution of musky in the lower United States can be traced back to this area. With stocking efforts on other waters, we have an abundant supply of fish. We can fish every day in different types of water with a wide range of structure—a cornucopia of musky habitat. And someone that is as endlessly curious as myself can never get bored. That is one of the things that keeps me ticking.

What has been the key to your success as a guide/angler?

Passion—it is a difficult sport and it is definitely passion-driven on my end. Musky top the list of fish that haunt my dreams. So the passion to chase and figure things out endlessly—even though figuring out a musky is thankfully an unattainable goal. I'm a curious angler and I enjoy learning and being challenged. And the muskellunge is a species that challenges anglers and asks them to continually raise their bar. What drives me mostly is the quest to fill up the knowledge base. But after 20 years I have more questions now than when I started. But that's a good thing because if it were different, I would probably go find something else to do.

What advice do you have for other musky fly anglers?

Take notes and maintain a journal. I keep notes on all my fishing scenarios and even information that I gather from reliable fishing reports. Experience is the greatest friend of the musky angler. So for somebody that is just getting into the sport—keep doing it. Take your lumps and learn. Every time out you have the opportunity to learn something new. Keep your mind open to learning from the fish, the water, and other anglers. And keep casting—time on the water is everything. If these fish were predictable, it would be a different game, but you never know when the time is that the fish will be active. Being out on your water as much as possible is the key. And you must be prepared both physically and mentally for chasing musky. You must be able to go the championship distance—to go 15 rounds—because there are plenty of times when the great catch happens right at the end. Those that aren't prepared can miss out. The truly great anglers have the ability to keep with it—keeping fresh both physically and mentally. This is a game of efficiencies and little fractional victories. It is a marathon and not a sprint, so having a little left for a kick at the end separates the wheat from the chaff.

What has musky fly fishing taught you?

It has taught me to dream big and to follow my inner voice. When I first hung my shingle, there really wasn't anything pointing anglers toward musky fly fishing. But my inner voice said this is cool—I love brown trout, I love steelhead, and I had some exposure to Atlantic salmon and these fish were sexy and exciting to me, but I had giant muskies in my backyard and when I figured out that they come beautifully to flies, I figured that people would want to do this. So for me this journey has been listening to my inner voice, and I have seen it go from a handful of hard-core practitioners only a few years ago to hundreds, even thousands, of anglers that are into musky fly fishing. Our brotherhood and sisterhood has hit a mass and is plugged into the pop culture of fly fishing. It has really been cool to see that happen, especially when some of the growth has been the direct result of talking about it, doing it, and promoting it. So it tells me that my little part of the universe is working.

Are you a sweet talker or trash talker?

Trash talker all the way—Reggie Miller. You have to talk to these things like you are lining up one-on-one against them and it's got to be a full-court press.

Describe a memorable musky encounter.

Looking back on the last 10 years, some really incredible things have happened. I have caught a couple line-class records and was part of a double catch where we caught a 47-inch and 51-inch fish at the same time. These were amazing things, but the ones that really stay with me are the ones that got away. And there are a couple of supertankers—50-pound fish that my clients have hooked—that we have been completely bitch-slapped by, and those fish go away haunting me to this day. So the ones that elude us are those that keep me dreaming.

Describe your preferred water and weather conditions, including other factors like moon phase if applicable.

For me the playoffs or the championship round comes down to the shifting of the seasons. The tipping of late summer into early autumn has become my favorite time. It used to be that the time right before freeze-up was my favorite, but as I have become older I am less enthused about the cold and frozen hands. I like fishing in shirtsleeves and chasing big, active muskies so middle of September / post–Labor Day into autumn is really my go time. What happens at that time of year is you quit hunting musky and they start hunting you. When the big fish begin to move out of the summer patterns, casts need to be right in their wheelhouse. Everything shifts as the weeds die out and the bait starts to disperse. Then the musky begin to roam and hunt. And when the musky are hunting, it becomes a whole different game. That's what gets me out of bed in the morning.

I like the periods before and after the new and full moon. I prefer the new moon. For midday moon rises or sets on the day or two before and after a new moon, be on your spot. Be on your big fish spot—these are definitely triggering times. Of course, local weather or conditions can trump all of that. However, the moon phases are observable items that you can put in your calendar years ahead of time. I also try to use approaching fronts to my advantage, especially after a stable weather period. I watch the activity of the birds and animals around the house when a front is approaching and everything gets active. It is quite obvious with the hummingbird feeders that I have around the house. They all sense something—so when the hummingbirds are swarming, it's time to grab the fly rod.

Additional Thoughts

There is no always and no never in musky fishing. If people say you can't do something, well, you probably can. Keep an open mind and don't get stuck in a rut. My greatest skill as an angler is being tenacious and irrepressible. Some of my greatest moments as a musky fly fisher were the result of endurance—being able to stay with it and keep the faith.

Blane Chocklett displays a solid southern musky.
BLANE CHOCKLETT PHOTO

BLANE CHOCKLETT

VIRGINIA

Blane is a guide, a fly designer, and a top professional in the fly-fishing industry. His innovative fly pattern designs have changed the landscape of musky fly tying. Blane regularly guides his clients to the musky catch of a lifetime on his bountiful home waters.

What attracted you to musky fishing with a fly?

Given my love for fly fishing, I would rather catch any fish on a fly rod than by any other means. And I have always enjoyed a challenge—so there couldn't be a greater challenge than taking one of the most difficult fish to catch on any type of tackle and to catch it on a fly rod. Part of what makes me tick is tinkering and figuring things out. That is what I enjoy about creative fly tying. So it was a challenge and I wanted to be a part of it—I wanted to figure it out and make it viable on a personal and professional level.

What type of musky water do you prefer or regularly fish and why?

In the South it is a bit different from what I have experienced in Wisconsin and up North. It seems like our fish in the South are lazy, since most will be located in holes and not in the transitional water. The southern muskies will use the transition water at times but generally will not be found in the riffles or in the side pockets next to riffles like I have experienced in the North. Our fish are generally in the holes, and depending on the time of the year, they move around within those areas. I prefer the winter when the fish are stacked in the holes. This also occurs in the summer, since there will normally be spring seeps in these pools that regulate the water temperatures. In the winter the entire biomass gets condensed in the deeper spots and the muskies have free rein over the entire area. This creates competition that can make the fish aggressive. Also in the winter the muskies are in a prespawn mode. The males are more aggravated, and the females are still trying to pack on a few pounds. So the deep holes are my favorite water to target.

What are the unique aspects of the water that you regularly fish?

Our mountain ranges here in the South are older, which has provided plenty of time for the rivers to dig out deeper areas. We also have big, long pools on some of our rivers that can have a length of a couple hundred yards to a couple miles. The fish will move around in these pools or holes depending on the time of the year.

In the summer the muskies will seek out spring seeps or cooler tributaries. Fish will congregate near the springs, and this is the best place to find summer fish even though they will normally not be too active during the day. In the fall as overall temperatures begin to drop, the muskies spread out. They can be everywhere, but nowhere in particular. I consistently find muskies at this time of year in the shallow, 3- to 4-foot areas of the pools that are typically barren of structure. I believe muskies move into these areas because the suckers and other food sources are there at this time of year. The suckers and other baitfish are most likely in the shallows, since this water will warm faster after a cool fall night, allowing these fish to regulate their body temperatures. In the winter everything moves into the deeper parts of the holes. In the spring the muskies will be found in areas similar to the fall, and we may locate some in odd spots as they move to the summer water. In the spring muskies will also be found in the tails of the pools, since this is where the suckers spawn. Spring muskies can also be found near brush piles and logjams since game species like smallmouth bass spawn near this structure. So when you step back and look at it, musky are almost always located near their food source.

What has been the key to your success as a guide/angler?

Time on the water and learning what make these fish tick by getting my butt kicked a lot. I have also used my experiences with conventional tackle—how the fish have responded to convention tackle to design the flies that I use. But you can't beat time on the water and having an open mind. I think that's huge.

What advice do you have for other musky fly anglers?

Stick to it, have patience, pay attention to what the water is telling you and to the time of year. And never give up. If you want to catch these fish, you have to be willing to put in the time. You can't expect to go out and catch a musky on the first 10 casts, but it can and occasionally does happen. You have to make sure that if your fly is in the water that you are paying attention.

I would also advise anglers to match their fly patterns to the food available in their bodies of water and try to choose the right fly pattern and size given the time of year and water conditions. In clearer water I use more natural colors in smaller sizes. When the water is higher with some color, I want bigger flies that push water and sometimes patterns that are more colorful. But some of my colorful flies are tied to match a food source. I use a pink color scheme a lot in the winter. And while I have seen this pattern referred to as a clown fly because of its colorful appearance, it is actually matching nature. As the water temperatures cool, the baitfish in my rivers—suckers, fallfish, chubs, and even carp—have a tendency for their skins and fins to start turning pink. So there is a reason behind that fly choice, and is a good example of paying attention to your surroundings.

What has musky fly fishing taught you?

It has taught me to be patient and to be willing to think more outside the box and to put my mind in the place of a predator by looking at things from their perspective. I relate muskies to cats—and to the way you can tease a cat into striking. Well, muskies are exactly the same way—they respond in the same manner as a cat. Both muskies and cats are very unpredictable, but you can also tease that unpredictable critter into striking. So it has also shown me how to use analogies in my teachings and seminars that others can easily relate to and identify with.

So when you have a fish coming in on your fly and tailing it but not eating, you need to tease it like a cat. You start taking the fly away from it—not fast at first, but just enough to make the musky feel as though it needs to speed up to keep up. I like to employ a crawl, walk, jog, run approach as I speed the fly up in increments. If you can get the musky to engage through those gear changes, you pretty much got it at that point. If you can get the musky in that mode, you are probably going to catch that fish. Again, like a cat. If you can begin to get it excited about that feather or toy mouse, you can usually get it to start swatting, then attacking. So I think the thing musky fishing has really taught me is to be more observant.

Are you a sweet talker or trash talker?

I'm both. If the fishing has been good and the muskies have been cooperating, I'll be a sweet talker. But if they are being difficult, I'll start talking trash to them and calling them names for sure. It's definitely a love-hate relationship. I hate them when I can't catch them, but I love them again when I get one in the boat.

Describe a memorable musky encounter.

There have been a lot of them—it was really cool to have you come down here to fish and to have that big one eat at the boat. I got to see that fish coming for the fly and let you know it was following before you could see it from your angle. I was sitting on the sideline and got to see all the action. That experience has really stuck with me. It all unfolded so perfectly. (Author's note: Blane is referring to my personal best musky. It was an experience I will never forget and one that left me shaking during the battle.)

Describe your preferred water and weather conditions, including other factors like moon phase if applicable.

I will tell you this—a lot of anglers like a full moon and I can't stand a full moon. I think the fish become very unpredictable. That being said, you can move some of your biggest fish during full moon periods, but overall numbers will be down. Muskies in my rivers just don't respond the same way as in the non-full-moon period. Overall, one of my favorite conditions is a moonrise or moonset, but particularly a moonrise, during the winter months. If I can get a moonrise in the warmest part of the day in the winter, I want to be at my best spot. I have experienced a number of days when we haven't seen a fish until that magical hour and then have multiple encounters. So I prefer the middle of the moon phases but pay attention to the moonrises and moonsets.

Big fish green is my favorite water condition. What I mean by that is water that is not crystal clear but is also not dirty—somewhere in between that creates perfect hunting conditions. The fish can't see your fly as well, so they rely on their other senses. And the fish are a lot more aggressive at that time.

Additional Thoughts

When stripping the line, I want the tip of the rod in the water. As the fly gets within 15 to 20 feet of the boat, provided you have proper visibility, I pause it ever so slightly to see if there is a musky following. This gives me enough time to feed a fish if there is one behind the fly. From this point it is critical to speed up the fly as it gets closer to the boat. The first turn of the figure eight should always be made by pushing the rod away from your position. Since a musky will often eat on the first turn, having it take the fly as it is going away from the boat and your position will greatly increase the possibility of a solid hookup.

Don't stop the fly when a fish is following—it is one of the biggest mistakes you can make. Also, it is so important to do a proper figure eight by speeding the fly up into the turns and by making big, wide turns so that the fish can see the profile of the fly. You want to show a musky that side angle. And you can't turn the fly back over the fish—musky don't get attacked by their prey. Also, when looking for your fly as it approaches the boat, don't be afraid to change the viewing angle to get a better look at your fly.

Eric Grajewski hoists a big musky he caught from his home waters.

ERIC GRAJEWSKI

MICHIGAN

Eric grew up in Michigan and was raised by two great parents who always had his family involved in the outdoors. He has fished extensively throughout his home state. Eric and his two brothers were featured in the fly-fishing film *The Brothers Brown.* He is now a musky guide and passionately addicted to musky on the fly. Eric's impressive self-made videos of his encounters, hookups, and landed musky will make any angler's mouth water.

What attracted you to musky fishing with a fly?

As a kid, musky always fascinated me but I didn't have much of an opportunity to fish for them. Around the time of my first boat purchase, I was really enjoying fishing large streamers for big predator brown trout. With a great musky lake so close to home, this seemed like a natural progression. On one of my first trips, I hooked a musky. You can say that musky hooked my soul because from that day on, I knew this is something I wanted to do more and more.

What type of musky water do you prefer or regularly fish and why?

I don't really have a preference. Because there aren't any streams nearby, I mostly fish lakes and a majority of that time is spent on one fairly large lake. I have enjoyed my time fishing in northern Wisconsin, especially the faster flowing rivers. Fishing trout-like water full of muskies is unique. To be honest, if a puddle held musky, I would probably try to fish it!

What are the unique aspects of the water that you regularly fish?

The water that I regularly fish is a large, open body of water that has very little traditional structure. What I mean by that is the lake is fairly flat, with the exception of a few rivers that dump in, creating channels. But there are very few rocks or land points, mostly just a flat lake with weeds everywhere. Structure consists of weed edges, water stain lines, or just locating forage in a vast open area in the middle of nowhere.

What has been the key to your success as a guide/angler?

The key to my success has been learning on the fly, no pun intended. Each time out you learn something from the fish. But as far as big water goes, I have found that boat control is a huge part of the game. Controlling boat position has a direct impact on getting the proper action on the fly and reducing the possibility of hooking yourself or someone in the boat. Discussions with my two brothers, who are both experienced anglers, have also helped shorten the learning curve.

What advice do you have for other musky fly anglers?

Be patient and seek out the information that exists on musky fly fishing. But keep in mind that what works for one angler or body of water may not work for another. Learn how to properly hold and take care of the fish so they will be there for you and others to enjoy in the future. Oh yeah, and fish wire for your bite guards. There is nothing more heartbreaking than seeing a fish of a lifetime swim away with your fly. Trust me, I learned the hard way, and fishing wire does not seem to change your number of hookups. That's what makes musky so awesome. They don't care. They will eat when they want to eat.

What has musky fly fishing taught you?

Musky will humble the greatest of fishermen. As soon as you think you have it figured out, you can go days without even seeing a fish. It's easy to get down on yourself or get frustrated. Musky have really taught me to enjoy my time spent on the water and cherish the moments when you hook up.

Describe a memorable musky encounter.

For a little background to the following story, I fish on a lake with a lot of traditional gear fishermen. And I see gear anglers land many large fish in the same exact areas that I fish. At this point the largest fish to hand for me was 43 inches. There was a time where I started to believe that maybe a really big fish just couldn't be fooled by a fly. Probably two weeks after that thought crossed my mind, I finally land a 46-incher that for me at the time was a giant. This definitely changed my mindset. Before the season had started, I set two goals: to catch my first musky on a topwater fly and to get a 50-inch fish on a fly. My next trip out after landing that larger fish, I ended up hooking and landing my first topwater musky on a fly. It just so happened that when I took the fish out of the net, it measured 51½ inches. I was able to kill two birds with one fly. I just drifted for about an hour after that, wishing I had a beer in my hand. It's a moment I will never forget.

Describe your preferred water and weather conditions, including other factors like moon phase if applicable.

I have the most confidence when the water is a greenish color with about 7 to 8 feet of visibility. Throw in some weeds or other structure, and it can be money! For me wind is the key—I prefer a nice breeze. Calm conditions can be difficult on my water.

To be honest, I am not yet a big believer in moon phases. What I have found is my five largest fish all came when a moon minor or major was occurring at the same time as a sunset or sunrise.

Additional Thoughts

I always want to stress proper handling of the fish. Most of us grew up learning to fly-fish for trout, and, as we all know, it is a sin to hold a trout by the gill area. And with most fish this is true. However, with musky it is very safe to hold them by the gill-plate area. There is plenty of room to get your hand in there without ever touching the gills. And this hold is the best way to keep control of a musky, especially a large one. Do I still do a tail hold here and there? Absolutely I do. But I see a number of fly fishermen blast people holding musky by the gill plate because they think this is an improper hold, and for musky that couldn't be further from the truth.

And a special thanks needs to go to my wife and family for letting me pursue my disease of musky fly fishing. Fishing in general is a stress reliever for me. Without it I would most likely snap.

Chris Willen holds a hefty musky for a client.
CHRIS WILLEN PHOTO

CHRIS WILLEN

WISCONSIN AND TENNESSEE

Chris is a passionate full-time fly-fishing guide who specializes in musky fishing. He splits time between northern Wisconsin in the summer and fall and Tennessee in the winter and spring months. He has musky knowledge beyond his young years and is becoming a well-known professional in the musky fly-fishing game.

What attracted you to musky fishing with a fly?

I started musky fishing when I was quite young in my home state of Illinois with limited success. In my late teens I bought a small boat and began to explore local waters. I then hired a guide that taught me a lot about musky, and from that point I hit the ground running. I was pretty much stuck on the musky game and didn't fish for anything else. It was when I reconnected with a high school friend in northern Wisconsin who had become a dedicated fly angler that my interest in musky crossed with his interest in fly fishing. After spending a couple months fly fishing for musky, I realized that this was the coolest thing I ever did. From there it has consumed me.

What type of musky water do you prefer or regularly fish and why?

When I first started musky fishing, I was a lake guy because we didn't have the rivers in Illinois. Then I moved on to rivers in Wisconsin. Most clients want to fish the rivers, and I like that as well. You are on a conveyor belt, and you know you are going to pass by a musky eventually. But there is still something about a lake that makes it my favorite water to fish. I like figuring out lakes—weed lines, bait patterns. The key to fishing lakes is to break the water down to manageable pieces. I usually focus on lakes when the rivers blow out. I like the variety of going back and forth.

What are the unique aspects of the water that you regularly fish?

The rivers I usually fish are absolutely beautiful, with little development along the bank. You may see only a couple cabins on a daylong float. And you don't see many other anglers either. When you are musky fishing, you generally don't want to see other musky fishermen. That's a big appeal to me—the un-harassed fishery.

What has been the key to your success as a guide/angler?

Persistence, time on the water, forcing yourself to keep going, keep casting and learning. Learning from every fish. And it's important to not take every musky as simply a fish caught, but as a piece of information about why the fish was there and how it was caught. This is what we love to do and it becomes a passion, but it is also a job and you have to treat it as such.

What advice do you have for other musky fly anglers?

Just keep casting. Don't let yourself get discouraged—it's a hard thing to catch muskies on a fly. It's a hard thing to catch muskies period. Just get out as much as possible and cast as much as you can when on the water. When something doesn't work one day, you have to try something different the next day. Get out there and do it, and do it as often as you can. The more fish you see and the more you interact with, the better prepared you will be to deal with encounters. Observe musky behavior and understand a musky's mood to determine the eaters from the followers.

What has musky fly fishing taught you?

The main thing it has taught me is that if you put your mind to something you can do it—whatever you want to do in life. Fly fishing has taught me to slow down. Slowing down helps me analyze structure. When I fished with gear, it was at a faster pace, but slowing down helps me fish effectively by methodically picking apart structure.

Are you a sweet talker or trash talker?

A little bit of both, and I think anyone that says any different is probably a liar. There are days where you are calling them sweetheart and baby and everything else, and there are days when you are *not* calling them that. But I feel that fishing angry is never good, so getting too mad at a musky isn't healthy for your fishing, but you need to stay a little angry to keep the edge. But as soon as one is in the net I never say anything bad—I am always so grateful. So I try not to talk too much trash.

Describe a memorable musky encounter.

I was with Brian Porter and a client named Murray Rosenberg from Los Angeles. Murray was being guided by Brian and invited me to fish with him. Murray has traveled extensively to fly-fish. While we fished I was fascinated by Murray's stories, one in particular about his techniques for fighting big taimen. Murray was casting to structure that was known to hold some big muskies, and I was casting aimlessly into the middle of the river, just enjoying being out on the water. I have always heard people say, "I thought I was hung up" when they hook a musky. And I have thought to myself, there is no way I would ever think that—when a musky eats I can tell the difference between a fish and a rock. So I make a cast and strip the fly and think, "I'm hung up." And all of a sudden I realize it's a fish and it takes off so fast that the line is ripping through the surface of the water, making that loud cutting noise as it ran upstream.

It was a healthy fish, super thick and 47 inches. It was beautiful—barred up and vibrant. But what I remember is that I had taken something from Murray earlier in the day. He showed me how he holds the line in his whole hand while retrieving and fighting a big fish instead of holding it with a couple fingers. So fighting this fish, I wrapped my thumb and whole hand around the cork. I couldn't let this fish run too much because of rocks and sunken timber, so I needed to stay tight and fairly close. It was a powerful, angry musky that kept trying to run, and I was fishing a 9-weight rod that was bent to the cork. I fought the fish using the whole-hand technique, and it made a difference. It was really cool for him to show me something.

Describe your preferred water and weather conditions, including other factors like moon phase if applicable.

Well, the full moon in October—that whole week usually is pretty good. But you'll talk to different people and they'll tell you different things about the full moon. I have had pretty good luck during full moon periods. Once the water temperatures start getting into the 50s, it is pretty much game on—it seems like they are eating every day. But when I get a nasty, rainy, snowy, miserable day, I couldn't be happier. That's when the big girls come out. With musky fishing you have the chance to catch the biggest fish that lives in fresh water. Those are the days that give you the best chance.

Additional Thoughts

The thing that I see people struggle with is the strip-set. Days are made and broken on the strip-set. If you're not strip-setting, you might get to dance with one for a while, but you're not going to get it to the boat. You can do everything else right, but it often comes down to the strip-set.

Happy angler Vince Tobia and a late fall musky that attacked his fly.

A Wisconsin musky thrashes at the surface.
BRIAN PORTER PHOTO

BILL SHERER

WISCONSIN

Bill has owned and operated a fly shop and outfitting business in Wisconsin since the early 1990s. He is considered a pioneer of musky fly fishing, catching his first in 1963. Bill has guided many anglers to muskies on the fly and over the years has developed a number of innovative fly patterns.

What attracted you to musky fishing with a fly?

I kind of arrived by accident. There was virtually no information on musky fly fishing, at least that I was aware of as a kid. I grew up on a lake and saw some anglers catching bass and panfish on fly rods. So I started fishing for bass with poppers, and one day the water blew up and a musky had grabbed the bass popper. This occurrence repeated itself even though most of the time I didn't land the fish. The first one I caught was just over 30 inches, and back then a fish of that size was a dead fish. You kept that fish. Everyone was encouraged that if you catch a legal musky that you eat it. So when I bring home this first fish, I was the hero of the day. No one could believe that you could catch a musky on a fly rod. I kind of got shoved into the back door by the muskies, but after landing a couple more, it was like, "This is really cool."

What type of musky water do you prefer or regularly fish and why?

I like water with muskies in it—in other words, water with good musky population densities. I really don't have a preference, for me it is seasonal. In the early season I prefer shallow basin lakes that warm up fast and provide good sight-fishing opportunities. Once we get into the heat of the summer, I prefer rivers. And in recent years I have been picking on smaller, out-of-the-way tributaries primarily because nobody else is on these waters.

What are the unique aspects of the water that you regularly fish?

We fish the youngest rivers in North America, since just 9,500 years ago this place was under a mile of ice. Our rivers haven't had time to carve deep channels. So a deep hole in these rivers is only 8 feet deep. Our muskies are real happy living in 2 to 4 feet of water most of the time and are only forced into deeper water when it becomes too cold. And our fish will readily move to follow the food. It puzzles me as to how a musky knows the precise time to move. I also like lakes because I grew up on a lake. A lot of anglers that fish rivers are afraid of lakes because they don't understand them—they can't read a lake. But these anglers miss some great opportunities from being too stuck to river water.

What has been the key to your success as a guide/angler?

I pay attention to the visual cues that nature provides, but I also have become a good angler by practicing it a lot. It is a lesson taught to me by my grandfather. And it really doesn't matter if it is musky, trout, bass, or saltwater fishing—I have become successful because I have studied my quarry. I look at what they like, when they like it, and try to get to the places where the fish will be feeding the best during those time periods. A perfect example is in the late summer or early fall after the first frost. Baitfish will begin escaping the shallows because it is becoming too cold and uncomfortable and they can't stay there. In the late summer the shallow water loses its oxygen, and the plants are at the end of their growth cycle and starting to die off. The baitfish begin to reluctantly leave the protection of the stumps and the weeds, moving into the deeper water.

In our lakes there are troughs that lead to the deeper water from the shallows. The baitfish are about 3 to 6 inches long. The muskies have not lost sight of this, and they sit in these troughs in the late evening waiting for the baitfish to come funneling down—it is free food. Why wouldn't you fish in those troughs? It took me a long time to figure out that this was occurring, but it makes perfect sense. So because of this occurrence I downsize my flies during this period. I have always attempted to bring a more analytical approach to fishing as opposed to just going out and seeing what happens. But the greatest thing I have learned about musky is no food, no fish. You need an abundant food supply. Muskies will move with the food, and the number one rule is that muskies will never be far from the breadbox.

What advice do you have for other musky fly anglers?

Stay to it, don't get discouraged—it is a very humbling sport. Some days it is just really good casting practice. But seriously, learn to cast really well. Don't follow the crowd and do what everyone else is doing—that will get you some fish, but it won't get you fish all the time. On really difficult days, like when a cold front has moved in, and I am out guiding, I know there is going to be a limited number of fish that are going to eat. So I have to manufacture a fish for my client. I have to find that one spot in that one part of the river or lake where a musky is feeding on that day. It may not be a monster, but it may be the only musky we see under those conditions. So I try to take all the little bits of information that I gather on the water to come up with a plan for that spot. That can really tax my brain. And if it taxes my brain with the years of experience that I have, I can only imagine how discouraging it is to those anglers just pounding the water and going through the motions. Step out of the box, step back, look at your habitat, and think, "OK, I'm cold and not feeling so good—this is not my favorite day out here—where am I going to go to find something to eat?" Start there.

What has musky fly fishing taught you?

Patience. There are a lot fly anglers that want to do this, but most fly anglers come from the trout-fishing side. And if you really want to catch muskies, you have to erase all the trout stuff that you know. It is really difficult to tell someone that everything they know is wrong, especially someone that might be a very good trout angler who has developed some poor casting habits in order to make the perfect cast on their trout stream. Some days I spend the majority of the time getting people to cast properly. And that is the most frustrating part of guiding. When you start throwing the heavier tackle, you have to do it right.

Are you a sweet talker or trash talker?

I don't trash talk. I am too old school for being a trash talker. I do think today there is too much emphasis on making musky fly fishing and a lot of other forms of fly fishing into an extreme sport. And we have lost sight of the lore, the legend, the history, and the gentility that fly fishing brought to the world for centuries—and we are talking centuries of history. There are some young anglers out there trying to make a quick buck and name for themselves, and they are trying to do it fast. It took me 40 years to get here. And we have to remember that, we have to remember the roots because that is what will lead us down the road. We need to remember the roots so that we don't make fly fishing into something it can't be.

Describe a memorable musky encounter.

I don't know how to pull just one out but can tell you I had a day when we landed 23 muskies in one outing. I also remember a day when we fished our asses off all day long without a sighting, and then 300 yards from the pullout we landed a 45-pounder. I guess one of my most memorable days is when I took a gentleman out who has become a very dear friend. He has macular degeneration and is legally blind, but he is a very good fly caster. On this day he landed a 51-incher. I can't tell you how good that makes me feel. He was ecstatic, and if he never catches another musky in his life, I don't think he would care. He is recognized by the IGFA to be the only blind angler to ever land a 50-inch or larger musky on a fly rod. I also took a woman out who was dying of cancer and she wanted to land a musky on a fly before she died. She missed three—she just didn't have the strength—and I thought this just isn't going to happen. Finally, at the end of the day the fish gods sent her one smaller musky and she stuck it and landed that fish. It was a great feeling for her. About a month later I received a letter from her husband that she had passed.

Describe your preferred water and weather conditions, including other factors like moon phase if applicable.

I like the weather when it is changing. If we have a falling barometer that's great because it will move the fish, but a rising barometer is not so good. Nobody likes a cold front—anytime you have a cold front approaching it will create more difficult fishing conditions. I don't like a full moon. If you are a trophy hunter and looking for that fish of a lifetime, fishing on a full moon after dark is a good idea. But if you are an angler looking for action, a full moon period is not the best time to be out, especially during the daylight hours. The time I do like around the full or nearly full moon period is on the moonrise. In the fall on the moonrise, it is usually late in the afternoon, but still in the daylight hours, I will catch a big musky. Sometimes it's more than one. The new moon is wonderful—I would take a new moon any day. Another thing that I found is the third day of whatever weather pattern you have, you are going to have good fishing, because it takes a couple days for the fish to get settled into whatever the weather pattern is. Unfortunately, if stable weather lasts for a week, the fish become stale.

8 MUSKY GEOGRAPHY

The musky fishery across North America is composed of a collection of intact indigenous populations, restored historic watersheds, and expanded ranges through introduction. Musky populations are commonly confined to specific drainages or waterways. Musky can be found in rivers and lakes of all sizes, providing fly-angling opportunities in a range of water types and an experience to meet almost any fly fisher's preference.

The calm after the storm—a musky is released after an intense battle. BRIAN PORTER PHOTO

An important 2011 research paper published by the Ontario Ministry of Natural Resources titled *Distribution and Management of Muskellunge in North America: An Overview* provides a great insight on musky distribution. Musky were originally found in only 12 states or provinces, with Wisconsin and Ontario possessing the largest number of rivers and lakes with historic native populations. According to this research, 26 states or provinces now have at least some water that is home to a musky population. Some of this expansion has occurred naturally, but most has been the result of stocking programs. This expansion has nearly doubled the number of rivers and lakes where musky can be found. Expansion is continuing in some states with progressive musky management programs. These figures do not include states that have only been stocked with hybrid tiger musky.

Expansion into many rivers and lakes has resulted in sustaining populations, and it is estimated that 73 percent of the musky waters in North America are sustained through natural reproduction. When fishing for any species, the experience from an aesthetic standpoint is generally enhanced when it includes interaction with wild, native fish. But when it comes to musky, rivers and lakes that are maintained or supplemented through stocking can provide an experience that is nearly on par with a natural fishery. Hatchery musky that have matured and spent numerous seasons in their home waters can be as difficult to fool with a fly as a fish that was produced naturally. A hatchery musky can also have the same appearance as a wild fish, provided it wasn't fin-clipped prior to stocking.

Fly fishing for musky can be confined to the experiences found on local waters or by visiting other rivers and lakes within a particular region. My own formula is to regularly fish the water at my doorstep throughout the season but to make regular treks to other areas for different water types and tactics or to extend the length of my season. I have always enjoyed the adventure of fishing new water.

If you live in or adjacent to one of the 26 states or provinces with musky populations, you are likely close to a quality fishing opportunity. Utilizing a guide who specializes in musky fly fishing is the most effective way to learn new water. Some musky guides who cater to gear anglers are becoming versed in fly fishing and can also provide a quality experience. It is important to fish with a guide who is committed to the

Musky are widely distributed throughout the United States and Canada. NICK PIONESSA PHOTO

fly-fishing approach and will not get impatient after an hour or two.

With the Internet, it has never been easier to research musky-fishing opportunities. State and provincial, fishing club, and chamber of commerce websites can all provide useful information on rivers and lakes, including details on specific musky fisheries such as management practices and access points. While serious musky anglers are typically tight-lipped about their fishing spots, word of mouth can also provide some clues, so always pay attention. We are in an era where musky populations have never been more robust and widespread, and new fisheries are constantly developing. Discovering these before other anglers can lead to tremendous opportunity.

The objective of this chapter is to provide a general guide to the North American musky fishery by discussing opportunities and management by region as well as focusing on specific waters that provide a quality experience. For the purposes of geographic coverage, the fishery has been loosely divided into three general regions: Northeast, South, and Midwest.

Northeast

The northeastern portion of the musky range includes the waters found in Maine, New York, New Jersey, Ohio, Pennsylvania, the eastern half of Ontario, Quebec, and Vermont. The Northeast region is home to numerous rivers and naturally occurring lakes, with man-made impoundments making up most of the musky water in Pennsylvania. The entire musky fishery in Ontario, Quebec, and Maine is composed of self-sustaining, naturally occurring populations. The management approach in New Jersey, New York, Ohio, and Vermont is a combination of natural reproduction and stocking programs, while populations in Pennsylvania are maintained mainly by stocking. The Northeast region hosts diverse musky waters, including large river systems and expansive lakes, smaller natural lakes and impoundments, and a number of smaller rivers that can be effectively fished with personal watercraft or even by wading.

While Quebec's musky fishery is sustained through natural reproduction, more than half of its musky waters were created through the introduction of the species. The most notable waters in Quebec are two of the larger river systems where musky exist. The Ottawa River, which is shared with Ontario, and the St. Lawrence River, which forms part of the border between New York and Ontario, are both home to significant musky populations. While both rivers provide the challenge of big, open water, they contain enough structure to be effectively fished with a fly. Some of this fishing can be easily accessed from the city of Montreal. The attraction of both the Ottawa and St. Lawrence is the size of the fish, as this is trophy water that consistently produces the largest fish in the Northeast region.

Musky can be found in approximately 60 additional bodies of water in Quebec, most of which are inland lakes within reasonable proximity to Montreal and Quebec City. Also, the lower portions of some of the tributaries of both the Ottawa and St. Lawrence Rivers provide musky opportunities in water that can be more easily covered by fly fishing than fishing the main river channels. Ontario is a haven for musky anglers, containing over 400 bodies of water that hold musky populations sustained through natural reproduction. Like Quebec, Ontario borders along the Ottawa River and a portion of the St. Lawrence, but the other significant bodies of water lying entirely within its borders make the eastern half of Ontario a prime area to chase musky with a fly.

The Georgian Bay of Lake Huron is one of the best areas in Ontario for trophy-size muskies and readily produces fish over 50 inches each year. The massive bay's points and coves provide the perfect habitat for musky fly fishing, and the Moon River Basin that flows between the Muskoka Lakes and Georgian Bay provides great structure and the opportunity for big fish as well. Eastern Ontario also boasts some good musky fishing on inland lakes such as Nipissing and the Kawartha chain of lakes that are in easy striking distance of the Greater Toronto area. The French River connects Lake Nipissing and Georgian Bay and comprises a series of channels, bays, ponds, and rapids that provide great fly-fishing water for musky and pike. Some of the waters of the wilderness area in Algonquin Provincial Park are home to musky that see limited fishing pressure.

Eastern Ontario offers river-fishing settings for musky that range from intimate waters to larger flows. This list includes the Spanish River that flows into Georgian Bay, the Saugeen River that flows into Lake

Ken Collins and Steve May with an Ontario musky.

Huron, and the lower Thames River that flows into Lake St. Clair. Located in the Great Lakes drainage between Lake Huron and Lake Erie, more than half of Lake St. Clair's surface area is in Ontario. St. Clair is one of the top-producing musky waters in terms of both size and numbers, and with relatively shallow depths of 10 to 15 feet throughout a good portion of the lake, it is perfect water for fly fishing.

While Ontario has built its musky fishery on natural reproduction and sound management, a reintroduction program is in progress at Lake Simcoe, just north of Toronto. In the late 1800s Simcoe boasted a robust musky population that was all but destroyed by overfishing and habitat change. However, a project fueled by volunteers and various funding sources is working to restore a viable musky fishery to this accessible lake.

Musky are not indigenous to Maine, but some self-sustaining populations in the northern reaches of the state provide great fly-fishing possibilities. Muskies in Maine are the result of introduction of the species into Lac Frontiere in Quebec; the musky were then able to migrate into the St. John River watershed within Maine's borders. While establishing a viable sport fishery, there are no plans to actively expand the musky's range within the state due to concerns over damaging existing native brook trout populations.

Musky now inhabit the St. John River, including the Northwest, Southwest, and Baker Branches, and a handful of lakes and ponds connected to the St. John, including Baker Lake, the first water to establish a musky fishery in the state. The fish numbers in some areas are impressive, and because the country is so rugged, there is very little fishing pressure. However, the harsh weather conditions of the North Woods result in a short growing season. Most Maine musky are below 40 inches, and the chance to catch a true trophy-size fish is somewhat limited.

Vermont's musky fishery is limited to Lake Champlain and a couple of its tributaries. Musky are indigenous to the lake; a self-sustaining population existed in Vermont's portion and in the Missisquoi River until a chemical spill in the 1970s destroyed the fishery. The Vermont Fish & Wildlife Department has initiated a stocking project to restore muskies to the Missisquoi River and Missisquoi Bay, with the objective to once again have a self-sustaining population. Numbers are on the rise, helped by Vermont's mandatory catch-and-release regulation on all musky.

New Jersey boasts a robust musky program. Musky are indigenous to over half of the state's 15 known musky waters, of which most are lakes or impoundments. The most productive are Greenwood Lake, Monksville Reservoir, and Echo Lake Reservoir, all of which are located in the extreme northern part of the state and provide good fly-fishing structure. The Delaware River where it runs along the north-central border of New Jersey provides the state's best river opportunity for musky. The musky fisheries in Lake Hopatcong, Mercer Lake, and Mountain Lake are continuing to grow in terms of numbers. New Jersey's stocking program reaches nearly all of its waters with annual plantings of both fry and fingerlings.

My home state of New York has a surprisingly diverse musky fishery that includes a wide range of lakes and rivers. Musky are indigenous to two-thirds of the state's musky water, and over half of these fisheries are still maintained through natural reproduction. One of New York's most notable musky fisheries is Chautauqua Lake, an elongated piece of water in the southwest part of the state. The lake once was home to a significant native population of musky that was nearly wiped out by overfishing and habitat destruction, and the fishery is now maintained mainly through a hatchery on the bank of the lake. Chautauqua provides good fly-fishing opportunities for a robust population of fish. The hatchery also fuels a musky fishery on a handful of other smaller lakes in the southern tier of the state, including Cassadaga Lake and Waneta Lake.

Two connecting waterways that form a portion of the western and northern border between New York and Ontario may best define the state's musky fishery. The St. Lawrence River, which empties Lake Ontario into the Atlantic Ocean, maintains a substantial native self-sustaining population of musky. The Thousand Islands area is a haven for musky fishing, and while it is vast, the islands and coves provide structure for fly angling. The St. Lawrence is known for its trophy-size fish and is the top spot in the state to find a fish over 50 inches.

The Niagara River connects Lake Erie to Lake Ontario and is also home to a solid musky population. Numbers dipped in the 2000s, but musky have staged a comeback. Due to the clear water and fishing pressure, the Niagara is one of the most challenging places to land a musky on a fly. The best fly-fishing water is in the upper river above the Niagara Falls, but musky populations exist in the lower river as well. The lower portion of Lake Erie around Buffalo can also produce good musky fishing, especially in the fall.

Musky fly-fishing opportunities exist on a number of more intimate river settings throughout the state. In northern New York the Grasse River, Oswegatchie River, and Raquette River, all tributaries of the St. Lawrence, provide classic river fly fishing for musky.

There are numerous lakes and impoundments in the Northeast with good musky populations.

A well-fed New York State musky caught by Ryan Shea. NATE CARR PHOTO

In the southern part of the state, the Susquehanna River and Chemung River boast good populations of musky that seem to be on the increase due to natural reproduction.

Pennsylvania supports an extensive musky program. While some of its waters were originally home to indigenous populations, a major stocking program has created a fishery in over 40 bodies of water while carefully extending the musky's range. The current goals of the state's management plan are to restore wild stocks and to provide a focused approach resulting in a quality fishing experience.

A good portion of Pennsylvania's musky water is concentrated in the northwest part of the state, including Allegheny Reservoir and Pymatuning Reservoir, the state's largest impoundments. Allegheny Reservoir is considered one of the best opportunities for fish over 50 inches. The other lakes and impoundments in this area vary widely in size, but some that provide notable fisheries include Conneaut Lake, Lake Wilhelm, Tionesta Lake, and Woodcock Creek Lake. A unique musky opportunity in the northwest corner of Pennsylvania is the beautiful Presque Isle Bay area of Lake Erie. Great Lakes–strain fish can be found here in decent numbers throughout the year. The shallow bays and islands provide great fly fishing for several warmwater species.

Lakes and impoundments supported through plantings of pure or hybrid musky are also distributed throughout Pennsylvania. Lake Arthur in the west-central, Cowanesque Lake in the north-central, and Rayston Lake in the south-central part of the state have the potential to produce decent numbers and larger-than-average musky on the fly.

Pennsylvania has some very good river fishing for muskellunge as well. The Allegheny River in the northwest part of the state regularly produces quality fish. Some of the best water is found below Kinzua Dam, stretching 30 to 40 miles. This part of the river includes some ideal fly-fishing water. French Creek, a tributary to the Allegheny, provides a small-river musky-fishing experience in an intimate setting, with opportunities for use of personal watercraft like a small pontoon or kayak and even good water for wade fishing.

Other river-fishing options include the lower Juniata in the south-central part of the state and the Delaware River where it shares the border with New Jersey. The North and Main Branches of the Susquehanna

A number of productive musky rivers can be found in New York, Pennsylvania, and Ohio.

River as it winds southward through the state provides pockets of very good musky fishing for both stocked and natural fish with the possibility of a true trophy. The outflows of some of the state's impoundments that have musky populations also provide good river fishing in the stretch below the dam.

Musky are indigenous to a handful of waters in Ohio. The state boasts a progressive musky program aimed at producing a high catch rate and trophy angling opportunities. The Ohio fishery comprises nearly a dozen impoundments, of which eight currently receive annual stockings, as well as some good river-fishing opportunities. The impoundments are spread throughout the state, with a slight concentration toward the northeastern portion. They vary in size from 1,000 acres to over 3,000 acres. Since most are in flooded valleys, there are numerous points, coves, and underwater structure to be covered with a fly rod. West Branch Reservoir in northeast Ohio, South Fork Lake east of Columbus, Alum Creek Lake north of Columbus, and East Fork Lake east of Cincinnati represent some of the more notable opportunities in terms of the size of the water and number of fish. A portion of Pymatuning Reservoir, previously mentioned as a Pennsylvania body of water, also lies within the border of Ohio.

Good river and stream opportunities for musky exist in Ohio as well. The Grand River, a tributary of Lake Erie that is better known for its run of steelhead, is also home to a decent population of musky and offers both float and wade-fishing options. Other rivers and streams such as the Little Muskingum River, Mahoning River, Paint Creek, and Sunfish Creek, which all flow to the Ohio River, are considered good musky fishing options. The Ohio River also provides musky fishing, but it is best to focus your efforts on areas near where tributaries with known musky populations enter the river.

South

The southern portion of the musky range includes Kentucky, North Carolina, Tennessee, Virginia, and West Virginia, with some limited opportunity in Maryland and South Carolina. The musky water in the southern range encompasses a much larger percentage of rivers than lakes or impoundments. Rivers and streams of various sizes provide a wide range of fly-fishing experiences, and the moderate climate of the southern range creates a longer growing season for musky.

Maryland's musky fishing is limited to the upper Potomac River. While not indigenous to the Potomac, a population of musky seems to be expanding through natural reproduction. The North Branch from Cumberland to the confluence with the South Branch and then downriver some 30 to 40 miles provides the best opportunity. The state also stocks hybrid musky annually.

Musky do not appear to be indigenous to Virginia, but the state has built a significant musky fishery that has expanded rapidly. The fishery is mostly supported through stocking efforts, though natural reproduction has become extensive in the some areas.

The best fly-fishing opportunities in Virginia probably lie within its rivers in the southern part of the state. The New River is stocked throughout its length in Virginia and is known for producing quality fish. The James is a beautiful, meandering river that is the perfect size for fly fishing. Musky have taken very well to its waters, as the population is increasing through natural reproduction. The best musky water exists above Lynchburg. The Shenandoah River near Harrisonburg and the Clinch River from Tazewell to the Tennessee border round out the lineup of good musky river options for the state. These southern Virginia rivers are fishable through the winter and provide a good option for a northern musky angler to chase away a case of cabin fever.

Musky can also be found in a handful of lakes and reservoirs in Virginia. Flannagan Reservoir in Dickenson County and Smith Mountain Lake near Roanoke are two of the larger musky lakes in the state, and both are stocked annually.

West Virginia is home to a surprising cornucopia of musky water, with over 100 diverse lakes and rivers with musky populations. While musky are indigenous to less than half, self-sustaining populations now exist in the majority of these bodies of water. West Virginia regularly uses progressive management practices with special regulations to enhance the fishery.

Both still-water and river fly-fishing opportunities abound throughout the state. Stonecoal Lake, located in Lewis County in the north-central part of the state, provides a picturesque musky venue. It is also known

Using the figure eight on a southern river.

West Virginia is home to a surprising number of musky waters. Here Jacob Ott works Bill Dawson through a productive pool.

for its large fish and is one of the better options in the state for a true trophy-size musky. Nearby Stonewall Jackson Lake, also located in Lewis County, is another West Virginia impoundment that produces consistent musky-fishing results. Burnsville Lake in Braxton County and North Bend Lake in Ritchie County are two smaller impoundments that produce consistent musky fishing.

Rivers make up the bulk of West Virginia's fly-fishing opportunities. The New River, which flows northwest out of Virginia through Hinton, may be the best known for both its length and scenery. It is home to some large fish, and fly-fishing opportunities can be found throughout. The Gauley River, which joins with the New to form the Kanawha, is also considered a top choice for musky in West Virginia. The Buckhannon River near Buckhannon is another good river option that has been improved by a special regulation section. While fish here may be on the smaller side of average, the numbers are solid and provide great fly-fishing possibilities.

The Little Kanawha, which flows through the northwestern part of West Virginia, and its tributaries host a solid population of musky. Both numbers and size can be found throughout the system. The Hughes River is one of the better tributary options and is perfect fly-fishing water. The Elk River downstream of Sutton, the Monongahela River, Mud River, Tygart River, and West Fork River are all above-average musky possibilities. Musky populations exist in Dunkard, Middle Island, Mill, and Sandy Creeks for a more intimate experience and even the possibility of some wade fishing.

Before I began the research for some past musky articles, I didn't realize that the original native musky range reached as far south as North Carolina. But musky are known to be indigenous to a handful of rivers in the western half of the state draining into the Ohio River basin, and with some introductions there are now at least a dozen rivers and impoundments in the state with musky populations. North Carolina provides a great opportunity for musky fishing in the winter months.

The French Broad River south of Asheville is one of the state's premier musky waters for fly fishing. The combination of annual stockings and significant natural reproduction has built a solid population. The French Broad is composed of good holding water and plenty of structure. The Lower Toe River in the western part of the state also hosts a respectable musky fishery. The Toe system can be fished with a small boat or kayak and also has water that can be effectively fished while wading. The Toe River meets up with the Cane River north of Burnsville and forms the Nolichucky River. The Nolichucky is also musky water that eventually flows into Tennessee.

North Carolina also has some still waters with introduced musky populations. James Lake, which straddles Burke and McDowell Counties, is a large reservoir with a good number of musky. It is also one of the better opportunities in the state for a trophy-size fish. Concentrating on the structure in the Catawba River or the Linville River arm of the lake will produce the best fly fishing. Musky can also be found up the Catawba River. Lake Adger, a smaller, picturesque body of water in Polk County, is another of the state's productive musky lakes. The Lake Adger fishery also includes the Green River below the lake.

While musky are not indigenous to South Carolina and there is no active management program, a spotty population exists in the Broad River in the northern part of the state. The fish apparently arrived in South

All smiles with a Tennessee musky. CHRIS WILLEN PHOTO

Carolina as fish moved south out of North Carolina during high-water events.

Similar to North Carolina, Tennessee also has a number of rivers draining to the Ohio River basin, where musky are indigenous. Today stocking occurs in most of those rivers to enhance or reestablish depleted numbers, but a fairly robust fishery exists within the state consisting of nearly 15 bodies of water.

The Collins River is located in the east-central part of the state and is considered one of Tennessee's top fisheries. It is a scenic river of more than 60 miles laden with good musky structure. Musky were likely indigenous to the river and were restored with stocking efforts in past years. Some fish continue to be stocked annually, but there is significant natural reproduction. The Collins River enters the Caney Fork just above the Great Falls Dam. The Caney Fork flows for 140 miles through the central part of the state and is stocked annually with musky. The Calfkiller River is another Caney Fork tributary with a musky population. This river provides a more intimate musky experience that can easily be covered by smaller watercraft.

The main musky still water in the state is Melton Hill Reservoir, located in the eastern part of Tennessee and part of the Clinch River system. Melton Hill is a run-of-river reservoir where the water passes through without long-term storage. The reservoir is stocked with musky each year, and very little natural reproduction is believed to exist. However, Melton Hill supports good growth rates, with many fish over 40 inches, and provides the best opportunity in the state for a true trophy. The Clinch River above and below Melton Hill also produces musky.

Kentucky is host to a significant musky resource that is composed of a dozen rivers and a handful of lakes or impoundments. Musky are only indigenous to a few of its waters, but the state has a progressive stocking program that has spread their distribution. Cave Run Lake is the best-known water in Kentucky and considered by some anglers to be the musky capital of the South. It is a 9,000-acre impoundment near Morehead and is stocked annually with a significant number of fingerlings. Cave Run produces both numbers and size and is a must for anyone fishing in the South. While a portion of the lake is big, open water, plenty of shoreline structure, bays, and coves are available to target with a fly rod.

Green River Lake is another impoundment in Kentucky that receives an annual planting of musky fingerlings. It is located in the central part of the state and is approximately 8,200 acres in size. While this reservoir doesn't grab the headlines like Cave Run, it produces consistent musky fishing.

A dam on the Licking River creates Cave Run Lake. The Licking below the dam and throughout its lower reaches is a native habitat for musky. The Licking River flows northwest after leaving Cave Run and enters the Ohio River near the cities of Covington and Newport, providing some of the best river musky-fishing opportunities in the state. The Green River outflow of Green River Lake also hosts a good musky population and like the Licking River is a tributary of the Ohio. Musky are most likely native here as well. The Green provides a more intimate experience, and portions of the river are quite scenic and undeveloped. The Kentucky River, particularly its Middle Fork, is another quality musky water that has the perfect structure for fly fishing.

Midwest

The Midwest area includes Illinois, Indiana, Iowa, Michigan, Minnesota, Missouri, Nebraska, North Dakota, South Dakota, Wisconsin, and the western half of Ontario. By any criteria, this area represents the very heart of musky territory. Some of the very best fly fishing in terms of numbers, size, the amount of musky water, and overall experience can be found here, particularly in Michigan, Minnesota, Wisconsin, and Ontario. These three states and Ontario are home to more than 85 percent of the bodies of water known to have indigenous populations of musky, and almost all of these have remained as self-sustaining populations.

Moving from east to west, Michigan is the first state in the Midwest area. Michigan has always been one of my favorite states to visit for fishing—mainly for its bounty of steelhead and inland trout. But it is also home to a large indigenous population of muskellunge. Over 100 bodies of water in Michigan have musky populations, with more than 80 percent being native, self-sustaining stocks. This makes Michigan one of the top states in overall opportunity.

Subdued—a musky is brought to hand after an energetic fight. NICK PIONESSA PHOTO

On the eastern border of the state lies one of the most prolific musky waters in its native range. Lake St. Clair is a 430-square-mile lake that lies between Lake Huron and Lake Erie. The St. Clair River drains Lake Huron into Lake St. Clair, and then the Detroit River drains Lake St. Clair into Lake Erie. Lake St. Clair is home to a significant population of native musky. The freshwater delta found at the north end where the St. Clair River enters the lake creates prime spawning water. And with good growth rates, both numbers and quality fish can be found, making Lake St. Clair and the Detroit River great spots to catch a trophy musky in the Great Lakes basin. From a fly-fishing standpoint, Lake St. Clair is ideal. It is generally no more than 15 feet in depth at any spot, and musky are typically positioned along or suspended above large weed beds or following schools of bait. Even though the lake receives heavy recreational traffic, fishing remains good through the summer and fall.

While St. Clair is the face of Michigan musky fishing, there is so much more to the state's resource. A number of other lakes also offer great fly-fishing opportunities. Lake Hudson in Lenawee in southeastern Michigan is a 2,800-acre lake that offers good numbers of musky and trophy regulations to enhance the overall size of the fish. It is an intimate lake setting that can be covered with a wide range of watercraft. Thornapple Lake in Barry County is a small, picturesque body of water with abundant vegetation. Thornapple has historically received a significant number of stocked fish, which is the main reason for its production.

Sanford Lake is an impoundment of the Tittabawassee River in the middle of the Lower Peninsula. The water here can run a bit turbid, but the generally shallow depths and shoreline structure provides for good fly fishing. Located in the northern part of the Lower Peninsula, Lake Skegemog is part of a chain of lakes in Antrim County. It is a relatively weedy, shallow lake full of musky structure. Numerous other lakes in lower Michigan are worthy of a fly fisher's effort, with many concentrated in the lower western or northwestern part of the peninsula. Many are smaller in size, but some are capable of producing surprising musky action.

Michigan's Upper Peninsula is a vast, undeveloped area with fisheries that have remained relatively intact from their original state. Natural reproduction provides solid musky numbers on many lakes and rivers, and the combination of wild fish and beautiful wilderness surroundings creates a unique musky experience. The Tahquamenon River system in the eastern part of the peninsula boasts great fly fishing and good numbers, though you won't find many trophies. The bays, coves, and islands of the expansive St. Mary's River along the northeastern edge of the peninsula provide a challenging opportunity to contact larger fish. Focusing on bait migrations can be the key to success on the St. Mary's. Productive lakes in the eastern Upper Peninsula include Brevoort Lake and South Manistique Lake in Mackinac County, both of which are just over 4,000 acres in size. More intimate lakes such as Kingston Lake in Alger County, Cusino Lake in Waybrant County, and Grassy Lake in Schoolcraft County provide a remote experience for native musky populations.

A number of good waters also exist in the western half of Michigan's Upper Peninsula. Lac La Belle in Keweenaw County is considered one of the better musky lakes in the Upper Peninsula, with a solid musky population and forage base. The Bonds Falls Flowage formed by the Middle Branch of the Ontonagon has a good population of naturally produced musky, and its general character of stumps, weed beds, and islands provide the perfect water for fly fishing.

The opportunity for musky in Michigan is about to expand into new waters. In 2010 the state began raising Great Lakes–strain fish at the Wolf Lake State Fish Hatchery instead of the northern strain as in the past. Fishery managers prefer the Great Lakes strain because the fish are indigenous to more waters, opening up the possibilities for stocking. The first crop of Great Lakes–strain musky were distributed to Lake Macatawa, Mona Lake, Muskegon Lake, and the Lower Grand River. The program is expanding to other waters, and some lakes previously stocked with northern-strain fish will be converted to Great Lakes strain.

Indiana's musky-fishing opportunities consist mainly of over a dozen lakes that are maintained through annual plantings. Native populations had disappeared by the 1960s, but with a successful hatchery program that has been in full operation since the 1990s, a vibrant fishery has occurred that continues to expand. Today's fishing opportunities have benefited from the cooperative efforts of local musky clubs.

Webster Lake in Kosciusko County is considered the center of Indiana musky fishing and provides the brood stock for the hatchery program. A connection from Webster Lake to Backwater Lake creates about 800 acres of prime musky water with a sufficient forage base to grow some big fish. Nearby Lake Tippecanoe is slightly larger than Webster Lake and is also considered one of the state's top musky lakes in terms of numbers and size. Lake Tippecanoe is known for its clear water and significant underwater structure that consistently hold musky. The Barbee chain of lakes also in Kosciusko County is another top-producing spot. The smaller James Lake rounds out the Kosciusko County musky water and is also capable of producing big fish.

Indiana is continuing to expand the fishery into a number of smaller, natural lakes throughout the state. Bruce Lake, located along the Pulaski-Fulton County line, is a good example. The fish may not be as large as those found in the Kosciusko County lakes, but the smaller lakes provide perfect size and structure for fly fishing.

Historical accounts indicate that some native populations of musky in northeastern Illinois were eliminated by the early 1900s. Today the musky fishery in Illinois is fairly extensive, with more than 40 lakes and impoundments throughout the state maintained through annual stocking programs. Musky-fishing opportunity continues to be on the rise in the state.

Many consider the Fox Chain O'Lakes as one of the best areas to try in Illinois. The series of interconnected lakes accounts for approximately 7,500 acres of musky water. The chain is located only about 50 miles east of Chicago in McHenry and Lake Counties, but despite heavy recreational use, the musky fishing can be very good. The lakes feature extensive weedy flats that provide perfect fly-fishing water. Also located in the northern part of the state is Lake Shabbona, an intimate man-made structure that was considered the premier musky fishery in Illinois before the rise of other fisheries. Shabbona has a plethora of sunken logs and weed beds that can be effectively covered with fly tackle.

Evergreen Lake is located in Mclean County toward the center of the state. It is a 900-acre lake with a good musky population where multiple-encounter days are possible. Following the changes in bottom structure is one of the best ways to locate fish in Evergreen. Farther to the south is Shelbyville Lake, in Shelby

Stocking programs have created some significant fisheries in the lower Midwestern states.

County. It is a large body of water at 11,000 acres and is becoming one of the state's top destinations. Shelbyville Lake features a wide range of musky structure and is one of the best places in the state to encounter a true trophy. Mill Creek Lake in Clark County is east of Shelbyville Lake and is in its growth stage. A concerted stocking effort has developed a good population, and a strong forage base has created the opportunity for big musky. Kinkaid Lake in the southwestern county of Jackson has a solid population and has long been the top choice of musky anglers in the southern part of the state.

With the ever-expanding musky program in Illinois, a number of other smaller lakes are well worth the effort. Discovering a sleeper before it becomes popular is a strategy that could go a long way toward successful fishing.

Musky fishing in Missouri consists of a handful of lakes/impoundments maintained through annual stocking. Pomme de Terre Lake is in the southwestern part of the state and is considered Missouri's prime musky destination. The man-made lake features 8,000 acres and a thriving musky population. Musky have been stocked in Pomme de Terre since the 1960s. Fly anglers should focus on shallow points and bays as well as significant changes in bottom contour. Fellows Lake is another southwestern impoundment featuring expansive weed beds and the possibility of large fish. Hazel Creek Lake offers the opportunity for musky in the northeastern part of the state. Extensive stocking has resulted in a good population with a high percentage of fish over 40 inches.

Similar to Illinois, the state of Iowa has put significant effort into developing a high-level musky fishery. The effort in terms of bodies of water is not as extensive as Illinois, but some quality opportunities have developed. Iowa's approach to stocking is fairly unique. Instead of planting fingerlings like most states, Iowa relies on yearling fish that have been minnow-fed in the latter part of their hatchery upbringing. This approach has resulted in greater survival rates and higher musky numbers, even after a reduction of overall stocking.

Big Spirit Lake in Dickinson County in the northwest part of the state is the largest of the Iowa musky lakes at approximately 5,700 acres. It is a relatively shallow lake, and most of its weed beds and sunken structure can easily be covered by a fly rod. Big Spirit has good numbers and the possibility of a true trophy. West Okoboji Lake, also in Dickinson County, is smaller at 4,000 acres but significantly deeper, with a maximum depth of 135 feet. This natural lake hosts a healthy musky population with the chance of some big fish.

Clear Lake is in Cerro Gordo County in the north-central part of the state. It was one of the first Iowa lakes stocked with musky when the program began in the 1960s. Clear Lake produces consistent musky fishing and is very shallow, with depths rarely exceeding 20 feet. Five other lakes or impoundments in Iowa have historically been supported through the state's stocking program. These include Lake McBride just north of Iowa City in Johnson County, Three Mile Lake in Union County, and Big Creek Lake just north of Des Moines in Polk County. The stocking program was recently extended to two additional lakes.

Nebraska is another state where musky are not indigenous but where refined stocking procedures have created a viable fishery. While musky were first stocked in a couple of the state's waters in the early 1960s, the fishery in Nebraska is fairly new, with many of its waters just beginning to mature. The state's fishery consists of a dozen lakes or impoundments stocked with yearlings in alternate years that are minnow-fed prior to their release in the wild.

Merritt Reservoir is in the north-central part of Nebraska and is one of the original musky fisheries in the state. The reservoir was created by a dam on the Snake River, and its long, narrow shape covers 3,000 acres. Submerged trees and weed beds that occur in its coves and bays are prime places to hunt musky with a fly. Merritt is capable of producing some big fish. Elwood Reservoir in the southern part of the state is another good option for musky. Elwood is smaller than Merritt, but its numerous fingers and bays create good habitat. Musky have only been stocked here since 2000, so it is a fishery still on the rise.

Nebraska's other rising fisheries shouldn't be overlooked either. Muskies are stocked in Calamus Reservoir near Burwell, Timber Point Reservoir near Brainard, Wagon Train Reservoir south of Lincoln, and Cottonwood and Steverson Lakes in the northwestern part of the state.

Both South Dakota and North Dakota have limited musky fisheries created through stocking programs as the musky's range is pushed farther to the west. Lynn Lake in northeast South Dakota is a 1,500-acre body of water with sunken timber and rock points and a fishable musky population. Nearby Amsden Reservoir is much smaller but known to be good musky water. Twin Lakes, or West 81 Lake, in Kingsbury County also has a musky population.

The musky fishery in North Dakota has some history, but its current program is still ramping up with stocking practices aimed at improving survival rates. North Dakota has only a handful of musky lakes, but within these lie the chance of landing some big fish. Lake Audubon and the Garrison Diversion chain of lakes in the north-central part of the state, as well as Red Willow Lake in Griggs County in the northeast, are included in the state's stocking program and represent a good opportunity to tangle with a musky.

Minnesota is known as the "Land of 10,000 Lakes" and for good reason. Lakes of various sizes cover a large portion of the state's landscape, and their number actually exceeds 10,000. Only some of Minnesota's lakes hold musky, and it is estimated that slightly over 100 bodies of water have a population of this toothy predator. Still, this is an impressive number and clearly makes Minnesota one of the top states in terms of musky opportunity. More than half of the state's musky waters are composed of indigenous, self-sustaining fisheries, but Minnesota continues to expand the musky's range by introductions to new

The aggressive musky engulfed the fly. CHRIS WILLEN PHOTO

waters. High minimum size limits effectively make much of Minnesota's water catch-and-release, further adding to the quality opportunities to be found in the state's bounty-rich waters. The state's management is clearly geared toward creating a quality fishery in terms of trophy opportunity.

A few of Minnesota's lakes stand out as top producers. Leech Lake may be the most well known and is located in the north-central part of the state. Most of the lake falls within Chippewa National Forest and the Leech Lake Indian Reservation. It is a huge body of water at over 110,000 acres. Leech Lake is very fertile, providing for excellent natural reproduction and good growth rates. Shallow bays in the early season provide great opportunity for fly anglers. Submerged weed beds and rocky reefs and points should be targeted through the remainder of the year.

Mille Lacs Lake north of Minneapolis is the second largest of Minnesota's inland lakes at over 132,000 acres. A good percentage of Mille Lacs fish are big, and the opportunity exists here for a true trophy. Fly anglers will do best focusing on shallow flats and rocky drop-offs along the lake's edges. Vermillion Lake is another prime musky fishery located in the state's northeastern tip. This lake also has big fish and features numerous coves and bays to explore as well as sandy shallows and rocky drop-offs. The Detroit Lakes area at the western end of Minnesota offers a variety of fishing opportunities. Musky were introduced to Big Detroit Lake, which now provides for a consistent fishery.

Quaint accommodations can be found while traveling through Midwestern musky country.

To the west of the Twin Cities sits Lake Minnetonka, a meandering lake of 14,000 acres composed of numerous bays. Fish are often located in shallow transitional weed areas, making it perfect for fly fishing. White Bear Lake to the northeast of the Twin Cities is a good example of a more intimate lake-fishing opportunity at around 2,400 acres. Lakes of a similar size make up a large portion of the state's musky fishery. White Bear has an abundance of musky along with good size. Weed bed and bottom structure provide for defined holding areas. Cedar Lake is another smaller body of water that features obvious weed lines and an abundant population. Sugar Lake near Annandale is also a quality fishery near the Twin Cities.

Lake Andrusia in the north-central part of the state has good fly-fishing potential along its shoreline weedy shelves. Lake Bemidji to the west of Andrusia is larger at over 6,400 acres. While its current musky population appears top-heavy and has fishery managers concerned, Bemidji has the potential of producing big musky.

With many more musky lakes to be explored throughout the state, fly fishers in the Land of 10,000 Lakes should only be limited by their own sense of adventure. The opportunity is here for an angler to find his or her own piece of musky paradise. As the state expands its musky fishery, the opportunity will only grow. Staying in tune with trends as fisheries develop could pay great dividends.

Minnesota's musky opportunity isn't limited to just lakes, as quality fishing can be found on moving water as well. The St. Croix River represents a good portion of the boundary between Minnesota and Wisconsin. Musky are indigenous to the St. Croix and can be found throughout, with the section from Taylor Falls down to the confluence with the Mississippi River the prime musky stretch. It is not uncommon to find some big fish in the St. Croix. Anglers should focus on breaks in the current, weed beds and edges, and fallen timber.

Beautiful musky rivers can be found throughout Minnesota and Wisconsin.

The Mississippi River cuts through the state of Minnesota and hosts a native population of musky. Most upper Minnesota lakes that are fed by or in contact with the Mississippi also have indigenous populations. The upper river provides an intimate, high-quality experience for musky. The section of the river from Brainerd to Little Falls offers some of the better possibilities for quality fishing. The section through St. Cloud also provides the opportunity for some big musky. The Rainy River and a couple of its tributaries along the state's northern border have a native population of musky as well.

There is little dispute that Wisconsin is the capital of musky fishing in the United States and one of the best states in which to catch a musky on a fly. More than 800 bodies of water in Wisconsin are estimated to have musky populations, and well over one-third of the musky waters of North America lie within the state's boundaries. That means that most of the lakes you drive by or rivers you cross while visiting Wisconsin will contain musky. Musky are indigenous to about half of these waters, with planned and accidental introductions spreading the distribution beyond its natural range.

One of the joys of fishing in Wisconsin is the surroundings and overall experience. The North Woods of Wisconsin are remote and expansive, and visiting this region transports you back to a simpler time. Constant reference to muskies at stores, lodges, and bars provides a constant reminder that you are in the heart of musky country. Some of the best fishing is found on picturesque rivers and lakes with limited development along their banks.

Musky fishing is serious business in Wisconsin, and in 1955 the muskellunge was designated the state fish. Resource management surrounding the fishery is also taken very seriously. Significant effort has been made to protect the resource and improve opportunities for trophy angling by raising minimum lengths, reducing bag limits, and adding other restrictive measures. Education surrounding catch-and-release and proper handling of fish is an important part of the long-term management approach. The state has rated its musky waters by angling quality and reproductive

Brad Bohen displays an aggressive Wisconsin musky for Blane Chocklett caught on a blustery autumn day.

status to provide a guide to the best waters and expected experience.

A section of a chapter of this book can hardly do justice to the opportunities that exist for musky fishing in Wisconsin, but certain destinations and waters stand out from a fly-fishing standpoint. Fly fishers tend to be drawn to Wisconsin's many miles of flowing musky water, by some estimates exceeding 2,000 miles. One could debate whether the town of Hayward or Boulder Junction represents the best starting point to experience Wisconsin's top fly water. Both towns are located in northern Wisconsin, surrounded by most of the state's musky waters. Hayward is in Sawyer County and has a population of 2,300. It is home to the National Fresh Water Fishing Hall of Fame, and throughout the town are numerous references to its beginnings as a logging outpost and its place in history with respect to musky fishing. Hayward is in striking distance of the Chippewa River, which is considered one of the state's top moving waters. With its East and West Forks, the Chippewa produces over 100 miles of musky water. Some of the better fishing is found in the 40 miles below the Winter Dam; however, access is spotty in the lower part of this stretch. The Flambeau River is a tributary to the Chippewa to the east that provides quality fly fishing. The water in Price and Rusk Counties provides the best fishing opportunities on the Flambeau, often flowing through undeveloped North Woods backdrops. A handful of other smaller rivers in Sawyer County contain musky as well.

The most well-known musky water in the Hayward area is the Chippewa Flowage, a 15,000-acre impoundment formed by a dam on the Chippewa River's West Fork. Its fingers, coves, and shoreline structure provide high-quality musky fishing and boast the recognized, but much debated, all-tackle record musky of Louis Spray. Other Sawyer County lakes with highly rated musky fishing include Grindstone Lake, Round Lake, Lac Corte Oreilles, Moose Lake, Spider Lake, Teal Lake, and Lost Land Lake. There is also the Eau Claire Chain of Lakes to the north and Lake Namekagon to the northeast, both in Bayfield County.

Boulder Junction is in Vilas County to the east of Hayward. The town holds the trademark as the Musky Capital of the World because of its substantial musky catch rates. Vilas County has only about half the musky river miles as Sawyer County, but a quality North Woods musky experience can be found on the Eagle River, Manitowish River, Turtle River, and the upper Wisconsin River. The upper Wisconsin has some wild, remote stretches with challenging water to negotiate. Boulder Junction is also within easy striking distance of the Flambeau River.

It is the staggering number of lakes that surround Boulder Junction that truly makes this area special. Vilas County has more than 1,000 named and unnamed lakes, covering over 93,000 acres. Many of these are home to populations of musky. Some of the lakes that stand out in terms of size, rating, and ability to produce fish naturally include Boulder Lake, Fence Lake, Flambeau Lake, Kentuck Lake, Little Trout Lake, North Twin Lake, Pokegama Lake, and Squirrel Lake.

While there is so much good water near, around, and between Hayward and Boulder Junction, the fishery is certainly not limited to this area. Good opportunities can be found throughout the state. The lower to middle stretches of the Wisconsin River around Wausau and Merrill represent a high-quality river opportunity for musky more centrally located in state. The Jump River in Taylor County is also considered a good bet and provides a more intimate river experience. However, from a fly fisher's standpoint, the joy of fishing Wisconsin may not be in its well-known rivers but rather in the miles of other flowing water to explore. An adventuresome spirit could go a long way toward finding lightly pressured, developing musky populations. The northern counties of Douglas, Iron, Lincoln, and Oneida each have at least two rivers that are A-rated musky waters. Other northern counties such as Ashland, Burnett, Price, and Rusk along with Clark County and Jackson County located farther south have 100 or more miles of flowing musky water.

The same could be said about exploration of Wisconsin's better musky lakes. While many of the best waters are concentrated in the northern counties, A-rated lakes are scattered throughout the state. Top-rated musky waters can be found in an incredible 40 counties in Wisconsin. This includes some larger lakes located more to the south such as the 23,000-acre Petenwell Lake in Wood and Adams Counties, Lake Wisconsin in Sauk and Columbia Counties, Lake Geneva in Walworth County, and Lake Monona in Dane County. But like the state's rivers, you can find peace and solitude on many of the smaller, intimate musky lakes—some that aren't even 100 acres. Some of these lakes are difficult to get to and have motor restrictions, providing the perfect setting for the quiet side of fly fishing.

Rigged and ready for adventure.

Wisconsin is also faced with some management challenges. A significant population of Great Lakes–strain musky was eliminated in Green Bay of Lake Michigan by 1900 due to pollution, habitat destruction, and overfishing. However, stocking efforts to restore this fishery have been quite successful and have resulted in a solid population of fish with good growth rates. This has been a cooperative program that includes the efforts of several musky clubs. Some natural reproduction is now occurring, but continued stocking will be required to eventually meet the target of the program. The stocking effort is also developing good musky opportunities on tributary rivers such as the Menominee, along the Wisconsin-Michigan border.

The western half of the province of Ontario contains some of North America's most productive musky waters in terms of numbers and size. Several remote locations offer a wilderness experience on pristine waters surrounded by undeveloped shorelines. Most of the well-known waters are larger lakes with plenty of visual structure to accommodate fly fishing. Musky are indigenous throughout this vast area of western Ontario that appears to consist of more water than land. Much of this water provides prime spawning habitat, and some of the better lakes are musky factories capable of producing significant populations even where fishing pressure exists. A greater emphasis on catch-and-release and the addition of more restrictive regulations have some lakes in western Ontario at their historic peak in terms of overall opportunity.

Lake of the Woods, on the border of Minnesota and Ontario, is considered by many to be the best musky water in North America. This large body of water sprawls over 900,000 acres, with more than 65,000 miles of shoreline, and is fed by the Rainy River, Shoal Lake, Kakagi Lake, and some smaller tributaries. Part the lake extends into Manitoba, but the portion within Ontario contains the prime musky structure. Most of the over 14,000 islands found within Lake of the Woods are in Ontario, and these islands with their numerous coves and fingers create ideal fly-fishing structure. The tremendous population of musky that exists here includes many fish of trophy size resulting from stringent regulations and makes Lake of the Woods a top destination. A number of lodges along the banks of the lake can complete the experience.

Bodies of water dot the map to the north and east of Lake of the Woods. Many of these contain musky populations, and some are very respectable fisheries. Kakagi Lake, one of the bodies of water that feeds Lake of the Woods, is approximately 28,000 acres in size and is considered another of the area's top lakes. Lower Manitou Lake is to the east of Lake of the Woods and accessed from Route 502. This lake is

A reason to be happy—success on a Wisconsin river. CHRIS WILLEN PHOTO

Many Midwest rivers are perfect for walk-and-wade musky fishing.

known for its high catch rates as well as the size of its musky combined with a remote setting. Gun Lake near Kenora is part of the Winnipeg River system and provides a vast area of musky fishing that contains various types of structure to be covered with a fly rod. A number of lodges and outpost camps are located on these lakes to provide on-the-water access.

This area of western Ontario is remote, and some lakes cannot be accessed by road. For these it is fly-in only. One of the most famous fly-in destinations for musky anglers is Rowan Lake. This is a wonderful musky destination. Rowan's fish are especially thick specimens that benefit from the rich diet that the lake provides. But best of all, this is a great lake for fly fishing, as presenting flies over and near fairly shallow weeds and reefs can be very productive. Focusing on shallow bays in the early season may even result in sight-fishing or topwater opportunities. Overall, Rowan provides a high-quality musky experience.

The city of Dryden, located along Highway 17, is in the middle of a trio of highly rated Ontario musky lakes. Eagle Lake is a 68,000-acre body of water to the southeast of Dryden and is considered one of the better lakes in western Ontario for big musky. Dryden is on the north side of Wabigoon Lake, which is known for high catch rates of musky and also for the opportunity to encounter trophy-size fish. Dinorwic Lake, southeast of Dryden, is also known for high catch rates. Dinorwic is attached to Wabigoon Lake through the Wabigoon River. Many lodges and camps also service this area.

One other remote and spectacular musky destinations is Canyon Lake, located northwest of the town of Vermillion Bay. The remote northern area is accessible by vehicle. The lake is nearly 8 miles long and has a range of structure including massive weed beds and rocky reefs and points. It is more of a numbers lake than trophy destination, though some big fish are caught here each year.

Musky opportunity has even pushed farther south and west with the introduction of hybrid tiger musky. Tigers are a cross between purebred muskellunge and northern pike. A number of states are stocking tigers in lakes and reservoirs to create a wider angling experience, including Arkansas, Colorado, Idaho, New Mexico, Montana, Utah, Washington, and Wyoming. The techniques and flies used for purebred musky are also effective on tigers. While reaching a size similar to a purebred, the tiger maintains some characteristics of a pike. Tigers tend to be found in shallower weed beds, and like a northern pike are quite aggressive. While pursuing tigers takes the same dedication as with purebreds in order to taste success, with a slightly shorter fuse, this type of musky may be a bit easier to bring to the fly.

I admire a naturally occurring tiger musky. NICK PIONESSA PHOTO

9 ESSENTIAL MUSKY FLIES

As fly anglers we spend a lot of time thinking about and even agonizing over fly patterns. This may be especially true of musky fly fishers. Since getting a musky to eat a fly can require every ounce of skill and persistence, the actual offering is often the final and key element to close the deal. For this reason musky anglers take their flies seriously.

This regal looking musky consumed a well-presented fly.

Decisions, decisions—trying to find the right fly.

The fly's importance can be overrated in some forms of fly fishing, and there are times when a particularly aggressive musky could be caught on a wide range of patterns. However, when spending hours on end in search of one fish, it is critical to use a fly pattern that inspires confidence. This gives you the incentive to continue casting even when the prospects look bleak.

When I first started musky fishing with a fly, very little information was available on tying big patterns. It was mostly trial and error, and with limited encounters per season, gaging effectiveness was difficult. But an explosion in techniques, materials, and sharing of knowledge has resulted in a new era of musky flies that are seductive, effective, and adaptable to a wide range of fishing conditions. In fact, some of the techniques that have developed in tying large, bulky, and seductive musky flies are spilling over into tying for a variety of other species.

Musky flies will typically be quite large. Muskies like to eat a meal. The typical musky fly will be 7 to 12 inches in length and tied in a manner that creates some bulk while in the water. This size is required to consistently get the attention of musky, especially big fish. Large flies also mean most other species won't be interested in the offering, so when a fish grabs such a big fly, it will most likely be a musky.

Choosing the right fly when musky fishing does not require the same analytical approach as when fishing for selectively feeding trout. However, using patterns that represent the size and color of natural bait found in a particular musky water is an effective approach. You should have a working knowledge of the abundant bait sources found in the water that you fish to help in the fly design and selection process.

The color of the pattern does not have to represent or mimic natural bait. Often a color combination is effective in a particular river or lake even if it doesn't represent something natural in the water. I suspect that such an effective color combination simply shows up well in the water or takes on the look of something natural underwater. But not being simply a selective feeder, musky are game to try anything once. I usually select patterns with more of a natural color scheme when fishing clearer water. I often go to dark-hued flies that incorporate black or deep brown when fishing water with a significant stain. Also, brightly colored flies seem to work better on bright, sunny days.

Most musky flies incorporate some element of flash. Flash fibers built into the fly can portray the lifelike appearance of prey as it turns and moves in the light. Flash in the fly acts as an attractant and triggering mechanism. I generally prefer a light to moderate flash element, but some patterns built with a lot of flash or none at all can also be effective.

Many anglers say that a fly's movement in the water is the most important element of a musky pattern. Seductive fibers that breathe, undulate, or even twist or spin attract a musky's attention. However, a side-to-side action as the fly is retrieved can be the most desirable movement, as it provides a musky with its preferred 90-degree attack angle. A fly that displaces water as it is retrieved tends to create this side-to-side action when combined with a hard strip.

Debate rages on as to the most important characteristics of an effective musky pattern. Size, movement, water displacement, noise, where it fishes in the water column, hook placement, and even whether to use a single hook or a treble are just some of the factors that most tiers consider. Barbless hooks are often used to gain deeper penetration into a musky's mouth and for safety if you accidently hook yourself.

In this chapter top guides and dedicated anglers share their favorite musky flies to help you build a repertoire of reliable and proven patterns for use on a wide range of waters.

A fly measuring almost a foot long was used to fool this musky.

BLANE CHOCKLETT is a guide, fly designer, and a top professional in the fly-fishing industry. His innovative pattern designs have changed the landscape of musky fly tying. Blane regularly guides his clients to the musky catch of a lifetime on his bountiful home waters.

T-BONE

- **Thread:** 210-denier Danville to match color of fly

REAR SECTION:

- **Hook:** 3/0 or 4/0 stinger hook
- **Tail:** 6 long saddle hackles, either all barred grizzly or a mix of barred and solid as shown in photo
- **Collar:** 2 separate sparse bunches of bucktail reverse-tied
- **Flash:** Holographic Flashabou tied in between and over bucktail collars

MIDDLE SECTION:

- **Shank:** 28 mm Fish-Skull Chocklett's Articulated Big Game Shank
- **Body:** 2 bunches of bucktail tied in utilizing Chocklett's Body Tubing for each bunch. Bucktail is tied tightly up to Body Tubing to stand material up and create the illusion of bulk with a minimum of material.
- **Flash:** Sparse amount of Holographic Flashabou tied in on top of each bunch of bucktail

FRONT SECTION:

- **Shank:** 40 mm Fish-Skull Chocklett's Articulated Big Game Shank
- **Body:** 2 bunches of bucktail tied in utilizing Chocklett's Body Tubing for each bunch in the same manner as middle section
- **Flash:** Holographic Flashabou tied in front of rear bunch of bucktail
- **Eyes:** Dumbbell eyes tied in on bottom of shank with Fish-Skull Living Eyes added to ends of the dumbbell with UV glue
- **Head:** Senyo's Laser Dub. This version of the T-Bone has a different color of dubbing on the top and bottom of the head, similar to a typical baitfish.

The T-Bone is an iconic pattern in the world of musky fly fishing. Blane's development and use of shanks has replaced the need for multiple hooks or tubes to create fly length. The shanks also create an enticing movement in the water. The basic concept of this pattern is to play to the attack style of most toothy fish by providing a side profile. With a hard strip and pause, the bulky head pushes water and combined with the articulation creates a jackknife effect. The result is a side-angle presentation and an enticing invitation to the predator to T-bone its meal.

The dumbbell eyes add to the jigging, erratic action of the pattern and allow the fly to sink at a similar rate to a sinking-tip. Blane's use of his Body Tubing takes the concept of a hollow fly to the next level by propping up a minimal amount of bucktail to create an illusion of a much larger fly. The tubing also allows the bucktail to maintain this shape for the life of the fly. Bucktail that is tied in using the reverse-tie method tends to flatten over time. Also, the bucktail is tied in mainly on the sides and top of the shank so the fly maintains neutral buoyancy in the water.

The T-Bone is as much a concept as a particular pattern. Shanks, Body Tubing, and a bulky head can be incorporated into almost any pattern, but the presentation of the full profile to a stalking predator is the key element that has made this pattern so successful for Blane, his clients, and just about anyone that has put it in his or her arsenal. The T-Bone is tied with just one hook in the rear section, but with the long tail the hook is positioned in the middle of the mass of the material—the desired placement for a side-angle attack on the fly. The T-Bone can be tied in any color combination. Blane has had particular success with brown and tan to represent the suckers found in his rivers, as well as combinations of pink to replicate the hues that fall fish and other bait take on during the winter months. ■

GAME CHANGER

- **Thread:** 210-denier Danville to match color of fly
- **Rear hook:** 3/0 or 4/0 bait hook
- **Tail:** 6 short saddle hackle approximately 4 inches in length, either all barred grizzly or a mix of barred and solid as shown in photo, with 12 or more strands of standard or Holographic Flashabou. The tail is tied onto the rear hook.
- **Body:** Six 20 mm Fish-Skull Articulated Shanks. The rear hook is attached to the loop of final shank. Two fairly sparse bunches of bucktail are added separately to each shank with a reverse tie. The length of the bucktail is increased for each section working toward the head. A few strands of Holographic Flashabou are added to the top of each section.
- **Front hook:** 3/0 or 4/0 stinger hook added by looping flexible wire onto first shank
- **Front section:** 2 separate bunches of bucktail reverse-tied, with a 3-inch grizzly hackle tied in to the side of second bunch to represent the pectoral fin
- **Head:** Spun deer hair tied fairly large to push water

Like the T-Bone, the Game Changer is a style of fly. It uses extreme articulation to replicate the movement of an actual fish's spine as it swims in the water. The Game Changer concept can be adapted to a variety of materials, including feathers and Chocklett's Body Wrap. Bucktail is used to size this concept as a musky fly. The pattern shown here is approximately 11 inches in length.

The bucktail on the rear shank is approximately 2 inches long. Each section going forward is tied so that the tips of the bucktail cover about half the material of the preceding section. This progression in size creates a fishlike profile in the water, as most fish are thinner near the tail and bulkier toward the head, and is critical to creating the desired swimming action of the fly.

The key to attaining the Game Changer's seductive swimming action is the head design. The head needs enough bulk to push and divert water, as it starts the movement of the fly. A bulky head creates a ramp to push water out away from the body and creates turbulence, which begins to then work down the body, as water naturally follows the path of least resistance. The push of water on the materials forces the shanks to move from side to side, resulting in the serpentine movement and realistic swimming action. A head that doesn't displace and divert will simply allow water to rush through the materials and will not obtain the desired swimming action.

As the name implies, this pattern has left its mark on modern fly design. Blane's creativity has resulted in a concept that will affect the way streamer-style flies are tied into the future. ■

WEDGE HEAD

- **Thread:** 210-denier Danville to match color of fly

REAR SECTION:

- **Shank:** 28 mm Fish-Skull Chocklett's Articulated Big Game Shank
- **Tail:** 6 short grizzly saddle hackle approximately 4 inches in length with a sparse amount of Holographic Flashabou
- **Collar:** 2 separate bunches of bucktail reverse-tied with a sparse amount of Holographic Flashabou tied in on top half of bucktail

SECOND SECTION:

- **Hook:** 3/0 or 4/0 stinger hook, added using flexible wire
- **Body:** 3 separate bunches of bucktail reverse-tied with a sparse amount of Holographic Flashabou tied in on top half of bucktail

THIRD SECTION:

- **Shank:** 40 mm Fish-Skull Chocklett's Articulated Big Game Shank
- **Body:** 3 separate bunches of bucktail reverse-tied with a sparse amount of Holographic Flashabou tied in on top half of bucktail

FRONT SECTION:

- **Hook:** 60-degree jig or swim-bait hook, added using flexible wire
- **Body:** 3 separate bunches of bucktail reverse-tied with a sparse amount of Holographic Flashabou tied in on top half of bucktail. A 3-inch grizzly hackle is tied in to the side of the third bunch of bucktail to represent pectoral fin.
- **Head:** Large spun deer hair head cut in wedge shape so that it is flat on the top and bottom, with UV glue liberally applied to make head solid and stiff
- **Eyes:** Fish-Skull Living Eyes added with UV glue

The Wedge Head is a combination of the T-Bone and Game Changer, taking key elements of each but using a head design that gives this pattern a unique action in the water. It is a multi-articulated design that can be tied using the reverse bucktail method or utilizing Chocklett's Body Tubing. As with the Game Changer, the Wedge Head features a short tail section since it utilizes four separate sections in a combination of shanks and hooks to gain its length of nearly 12 inches.

The Wedge Head features two hooks: one in the middle, which is Blane's preference for hook placement, and one in the front. The hook in the front is the key to the fly's enticing action. The deer hair head is spun on the down-angle section of the hook shank. The idea for this style of head is borrowed from well-known Michigan guide and fly designer Tommy Lynch and is featured in his Drunken Disorderly streamer pattern. The large, flat head digs and pitches left and right as the fly is retrieved, creating the enticing movement of a baitfish in distress. It has an uneven look in the water like a Rapala but with the swimming action of a Game Changer.

This pattern has resulted in a number of exciting takes and encounters for Blane and his clients over the years. Blane has found that the action of this fly can result in a solid take from musky that had been neutral to other patterns. The Wedge Head shows itself as something different and offbeat, which can be effective on musky that receive heavy fishing pressure. ■

BRAD BOHEN owns and operates Musky Country Outfitters in northern Wisconsin, guiding fly fishers to the diverse musky waters of the area. He was also featured in the fly-fishing film *Zero to Hero*, which explores the passion and zaniness of musky fly fishing. Brad is considered one of the pioneers and the top ambassador of musky fly fishing, and his work has helped popularize this form of the sport.

BUFORD

- **Hook:** 3/0 Gamakatsu trailer hook
- **Thread:** 210-denier Danville to match color of fly
- **Tail:** Long bucktail tied in around hook shank and healthy amount of Holographic Flashabou extending past the end of bucktail tied in on top of hook shank. The bucktail acts as a keel and protects the hook from fouling with the saddle hackle and flash.
- **Hackle:** 4 long barred saddle hackle tied in on top and to side of hook shank extending past the end of Flashabou
- **Wing:** Long bucktail reverse-tied to create a higher profile topped with a sparse amount of Flashabou and Krystal Flash
- **Head:** Deer hair spun and trimmed with a tapered effect that is smallest at the eye of hook and larger toward the rear. The fly is not designed to fish on the surface, so the deer hair is not packed tight. Some of the tips of the spun deer hair can remain untrimmed to create a collar.

I had the pleasure of watching Brad tie a Buford on a beautiful late September morning along the banks of Wisconsin's Flambeau River. The flow of the water outside the window with the early morning sun dancing off the riffles inspired his selection of materials. Tying in such a setting allows for creating a fly with soul.

Key to the success of this pattern is the reduction of materials to essential elements. The pattern creates silhouette and movement without bulk. It is easy to cast on a daylong outing, while proving to be extremely effective on musky throughout their range. In the water this pattern presents itself with an enticing movement. The spun deer head pushes water, creating an erratic action with a strip-and-pause retrieve.

This fly is considered Brad's signature pattern, used to explore the musky waters of Wisconsin. Watching him tie this pattern, I was surprised at its simplicity; however, each tying step was done with meticulous care. Brad explains that he puts the same care into a fly that he would in preparing a meal, since in essence you are preparing a meal—for a vicious predator. ■

HANG TIME OPTIC MINNOW

- **Hook:** 3/0 Gamakatsu trailer hook
- **Thread:** 210-denier Danville to match color of fly
- **Tail:** Long bucktail tied in around hook shank and a healthy amount of Holographic Flashabou extending well past the end of bucktail tied in on top of hook shank. The bucktail acts as a keel and protects the hook from fouling with the saddle hackle and flash.
- **Hackle:** 2 saddle hackles tied in on each side to complement color scheme of fly
- **Wing:** Long bucktail reverse-tied to create illusion of bulk. There should be enough room on the hook shank to add 4 or 5 layers of bucktail; using 2 or 3 colors can create the color scheme of the popular bait of any water. A sparse amount of Krystal Flash is added under the bucktail. Two short saddle hackles tied on top of hook shank are optional.
- **Eyes:** 3-D eyes
- **Head:** Heavy coating of Clear Cure Goo with the eye angling in toward the eye of hook

Like the Buford, this pattern can be tied easily with a minimum of materials. To add the Flashabou for the tail, Brad cuts off a long length and ties it down at about two-thirds the length, folding the shorter end over and lashing it all down with the thread. This secures the fibers if a musky just grabs the tail of the fly.

Bucktail is the key to Brad's flies, and he stresses the use of quality material with long, flowing fibers. The bucktail is added by cutting an amount from the tail and combing out under fibers. The amount used shouldn't be too bulky but enough to evenly cover the hook shank. Tie the bucktail down on top of the shank, tips pointing forward, with three loose wraps and then slowly tighten the wrap, allowing the bucktail to flare and move around the shank. Additional thread wraps in front of the bucktail forces it to flow toward the rear of the fly. ■

747

REAR SECTION:

- **Hook:** 4/0 or 5/0 Gamakatsu 55014 spinnerbait hook
- **Thread:** 210-denier Danville to match color of fly
- **Tail:** Bucktail tied in around hook shank and a healthy amount of standard and Holographic Flashabou extending well past the end of bucktail. The bucktail acts as a keel and protects the hook from fouling with the saddle hackle and flash.
- **Hackle:** 4 long barred saddle hackle tied in on top and to the side of hook shank extending past the end of Flashabou
- **Wing:** Sparse amount of Krystal Flash under reverse-tied bucktail

FRONT SECTION:

- **Shank:** Homemade shank using .051-inch stainless steel wire approximately 2 inches in length
- **Thread:** 210-denier Danville to match color of fly
- **Wing:** 3 layers of reverse-tied bucktail with Krystal Flash and 4 short saddle hackles mixed in between the layers
- **Head:** Deer hair spun and trimmed with a tapered effect that is smallest at the eye of hook and larger toward the rear. The fly is not designed to fish on the surface, so the deer hair is not packed tight.
- **Connection:** The two sections are connected with an split ring attached to the hook shank and a barrel swivel built into the rear eye of the shank.

The 747 pulls tying steps from both the Buford and Hang Time to create a slightly longer jointed version of a musky fly. By combining a split ring with a barrel swivel for the connection and a spun deer hair head, the fly has an enticing swimming movement in the water when retrieved.

A ring is created at both ends to form the shank. Two turns of wire are then wrapped back on the main length, securing the loop. Any excess wire is trimmed. The 747 can be tied out to 12 inches in length, but as with Brad's other patterns, a minimum of materials allows the fly to be cast with relative ease. ■

LARRY DAHLBERG needs no introduction. He has spent his life in the fishing industry as a guide, writer, tackle innovator, and television personality. His adventures on his show, *The Hunt for Big Fish*, have entertained us for years.

DAHLBERG MEGA DIVER

Tied by Charlie Dickson

- **Hook:** 2/0 to 4/0 straight eye
- **Thread:** Gudebrod GX2 to match color of fly
- **Weed guard (optional):** 80-pound hard mono
- **Tail/body:** Big Fly Fiber and Flashabou
- **Head:** Deer hair spun and trimmed, tapering to the eye of hook with a large collar at the rear of head
- **Eyes:** 3D Molded Eyes

Well before the creation of most of the flies that we now use to fish for musky there was the Dahlberg Mega Diver. Larry designed this pattern 40 years ago to fish for pike and musky with a fly rod. The fly is designed to dive underwater when stripped and pop back toward the surface during the pause, an erratic motion that induces savage strikes from musky. While the fly can be fished on a floating or intermediate line, the action is exaggerated when combined with a medium sink rate sinking-tip. This pattern is most effective when musky are in water 10 feet or less in depth.

Big Fly Fiber was one of the first synthetic winging materials available for big flies. Larry selected this material because its length and lightness allows for the creation of a 10-inch fly with the illusion of bulk, giving the fly the overall appearance of a meal for a musky. But because a fairly sparse amount of Big Fly Fiber is needed to create the tail/body, the fly remains fairly light and streamlined, allowing it to be easily cast significant distances.

The Mega Diver is not difficult to tie but will take some practice to perfect, especially if you are new to spinning deer hair. A small to medium bunch of Big Fly Fiber along with a dozen or so strands of Flashabou will take care of the tail/body. The front three-quarters of the hook will be covered with the spun deer hair head. The deer hair should be packed tight and tied in with the tips facing the rear.

The key to finishing the fly is properly trimming the deer hair to form the diving head. Carefully use a sharp razorblade for the trimming. Trim the bottom flat, being careful not to cut too close to the hook shank and risk slicing the tying thread. The top and sides should be trimmed tapered toward the hook eye. Form the collar by not trimming the hair on the top and sides all the way back. The collar is key to the fly diving and plowing under the water, creating a bubble line. The collar should be trimmed across the top to even the tips. A thorough coat of Dave's Flexament prevents the deer hair from absorbing too much water when it is fished and stiffens the collar to improve its performance. Foam diver heads are available on the market that simplify the tying process but generally don't perform as well as the spun deer hair head. ■

NICK PIONESSA is a professional guide, fly tier, and photographer. And in recent years, he has become a dedicated musky angler.

SUPER SWIMMY

- **Tube:** Large HMH Poly Tube, 2-3 inches for an 8- to 9-inch fly either clear or to match general color scheme of fly
- **Thread:** 210-denier Danville to match color of fly
- **Tail section:** Body color Slinky Fibre tied in at one quarter of the length of the fiber 360 degrees around the tube, then fold the front three quarters of the fiber back and dam with thread. Make several turns of crystal Antron chenille on top of each other to create a flare bump. Tie in 3-4 body-colored schlappen feathers on each side of the tube right in front of the bump; tie near the base of the stem so they flare out as much as possible. Add 2 more back-colored saddle or schlappen feathers tied in flat on top.
- **Body and mid-wing flare bump:** Crystal Antron chenille
- **Mid-wing/body:** Steve Farrar's Flash Blend or Slinky Fibre reverse-tied 360 degrees; belly color
- **Mid overwing:** Reverse-tied Steve Farrar's Flash Blend on top, longer than body fiber; back color
- **Flash:** Holographic Flashabou
- **Body and front wing flare bump:** Crystal Antron chenille
- **Front wing/body:** Steve Farrar's Flash Blend or Slinky Fibre reverse-tied 360 degrees
- **Eyes:** 5/16 Real Eyes Plus tied in on bottom of tube
- **Flash:** Holographic Flashabou
- **Front overwing:** Reverse-tied Farrar blend on top, long enough to reach just short of longest tail hackle
- **Body hackles:** Flared saddle or schlappen, 2-3 per side, long enough to reach base of tail hackles
- **Topping:** About 6 long, thin saddle hackles or ostrich strands centered over wing and a bit longer than entire fly

This fly originated as basically a large Clouser Minnow tied on a tube. As the size of the fly grew, a modification was needed to increase diameter and overall bulk of the fly. Two sections made for enough bulk for flies in the 6-inch range. When it was expanded to longer than 8 inches, it was clear another section was needed to maintain the profile. "I was getting a good swim effect to the fly but not as much as I wanted," says Nick. "Synthetics typically do not have a lot of motion, so I then began to add saddles and Flashabou along the sides and it became super swimmy. Not the snakelike, side-to-side action so common in musky flies, but more of a controlled shimmy down the entire fly. To my eye it's more realistic of a baitfish."

With the use of a plastic tube and only one hook, the fly is lighter than most and also resistant to forward motion in the water. When stripped hard and short, it darts, then jackknifes as it stops, then darts again as it's stripped hard. If stripped normally or with a two-handed technique, the fly swims and breathes. The fly is relatively light despite the dumbbell eyes, which help the fly orientate properly. It is an easy fly to cast compared to some bucktail patterns and allows for the use of lighter rods where applicable. ■

SHUTTLECOCK

- **Tube:** Large HMH Poly Tube, 3 inches either clear or to match general color scheme of fly
- **Thread:** 210-denier Danville to match color of fly
- **Butt:** Ball of dubbing to flare tail and hackles
- **Tail:** Small section of Supreme Hair tied in and reversed against dubbing ball; 6-10 long hackles splayed away from center with their natural curve, tied in 360 degrees around tube; Flashabou of desired color and amount
- **Body:** Alternating colors of Supreme Hair reverse-tied and flared as described below
- **Body flash:** Flashabou of desired color and amount
- **Head:** Supreme Hair reversed and flared 3 times tightly together and larger than body flares to create a large-profile head to provide resistance and make the fly wobble
- **Eyes:** Stick-on eyes coated with several coats of UV-cure glue

The Shuttlecock features a unique tying step developed by Nick in order to tie big flies from synthetics as opposed to bucktail. The idea was inspired by the use of flex cord or tubing to prop up a reverse-tied bucktail. The synthetic material is first tied in near the butt of the material, with the tip end pointed forward, and spread evenly around the tube. The material is pulled back and the thread is wrapped forward about a half inch; this distance can vary to determine the size of the material flare. The material is pulled forward and two wraps are made around it. From the second tie-down point the material is pushed back to the original tie-down point, creating a flare or swell. The material is then bound in place with several wraps.

To make the material flare stiff and secure, the area is coated with UV glue. The tips of the synthetic material are then pulled back evenly around the tube and tied down with thread covering the material at the base of the reversal to force the material to the rear. This allows the synthetic wing to flare and stand up, creating the illusion of bulk while limiting the overall amount of material.

The best retrieve for this pattern is the standard hard strip and pause so that the fly darts forward then jackknifes from the resistance created by the shape of the head. This retrieve also makes the tail wag and flash while giving a general look of distress. The Shuttlecock wobbles nicely on a two-hand strip.

Nick developed this fly to create a lifelike wobble while being row-trolled by our friend Bill Ingersoll. With a row troll it is impossible to row hard enough to mimic the hand strip, but the pulse of the oar stroke was enough to give the fly an erratic movement. Nick has also experimented with a multi-shank articulated version similar to Blane Chocklett's Game Changer style. In lighter colors the synthetic hair is more translucent compared to bucktail. ■

STEVE WASCHER is a commercial fly tier and fly-fishing sales representative living along some top musky water in southwestern New York State. Steve is a high-quality tier, and his innovative designs have been catching muskies for years.

ESOXULATOR

- **Main hook:** 5/0 Owner spinnerbait 5320 or Gamakatsu SP11-3L3H
- **Stinger hook:** 2/0-4/0 Owner 5111 or 2/0-5/0 Gamakatsu Octopus 0241
- **Tailing wire:** 45-pound, .028-diameter Mason NyloStrand. Use 10 inches of wire to form a loop to the rear of the front hook that extends 3 inches beyond the bend.
- **Thread:** 210-denier Wapsi UTC or Danville Flat Waxed Nylon to match color of the fly
- **Weight:** Medium or large conehead added to the top of front hook approximately ⅓ of the way back from hook eye by threading the wire used to attach rear hook through conehead up to the eye and then back along hook shank. The wire is lashed down with thread and coated with glue.
- **Glues:** Superglue for securing wire onto hook shank, Fly Rite for all tying applications, Zap-A-Gap for gluing eyes to fly body, Bond 527 or silicone for head and throat of fly

REAR SECTION:

- **Tail:** 6 long olive grizzly saddle hackles and 4 long gray saddle hackles with a sparse amount of Krinkle Mirror Flash and large Flashabou
- **Flank:** 2 olive grizzly hen hackles over 2 white hen hackles on each side tied to splay out

MIDDLE SECTION:

- **Tube:** 1½-inch section of ⅛-inch plastic tube fly material
- **Body:** EP Sparkle Brush, olive over green

FRONT SECTION:

- **Wing and flank:** Strung Fuzzy Fiber in contrasting colors to include white for throat and olive for back/wing. After advancing the thread past the conehead, cut a ½-inch-wide piece of white Strung Fuzzy Fiber. Fold material in half and cut it at halfway point, then tie it in approximately ⅜ inch behind eye of hook on the underside of shank with ⅔ of the material extending forward. Repeat this process, adding Strung Fuzzy Fiber to top and flank of hook shank, making sure that tips align at front. Fold material back and build a small head between material and eye of hook.
- **Crest:** Peacock Angel Hair folded and added in the same manner as Strung Fuzzy Fiber
- **Eyes:** 3D eyes, 7.5 to 15 mm depending on fly size. Tie in the mono of the 3D eyes positioned approximately ½ inch behind hook eye. Use Zap-A-Gap on back side of eyes and press together with your fingers.
- **Finish:** Attach rear section to front section. Apply Bond 527 or silicone to the front of the fly back and over the eyes.

Steve's pattern has proven to be very effective on the waters of New York's southern tier and beyond. He created it nearly 15 years ago to address his need for an effective musky fly to fish local waters. The inspiration for the Esoxulator came from Bob Popovics's Shady Lady squid pattern, which is tied on monofilament stretched between two vises to form the tail that allows the rear section of the fly to swing freely. While this is a great method to gain movement, it is a time-consuming step and didn't allow for a stinger hook. Steve solved the problem by using a tube for the rear section.

Using the modular approach to the pattern allows for the control of variables. Nearly every aspect of the

fly can be adjusted, allowing for a variety of shapes and sizes. One of the final adjustments to the fly was adding the conehead to the shank of the front hook. The weight gives the fly a unique listing motion upon rest, resembling prey that is dying and vulnerable. Folding back the winging material gives the fly a conical formation that produces more resistance as it tracks through the water. This style of head also results in enhanced tail movement without the need to manually impart action to the fly. ■

MATT GRAJEWSKI is an accomplished musky fly angler from Michigan who ties effective musky patterns. His flies are available for sale through custom orders. Matt appeared with his two brothers in the fly-fishing film *The Brothers Brown.*

YARD SALE

- **Rear hook:** 5/0 spinnerbait hook
- **Thread:** 210-denier Danville to match color of fly
- **Rattle:** Large plastic rattle
- **Tail:** Hackle or schlappen feathers and Holographic Flashabou
- **Rear body:** Flash 'N Slinky stacked on top and bottom, with a ¼-inch gap between stacks; Holographic Flashabou tied in on sides
- **Wing:** Craft Fur and Flashabou
- **Connection:** 60-pound Steelon (coated wire)
- **Front hook:** 6/0 spinnerbait hook
- **Front body:** Flash 'N Slinky stacked on top and bottom, with a ¼-inch gap between stacks; Flashabou tied on sides
- **Wing:** Craft Fur and Holographic Flashabou
- **Head:** Laser Dub stacked on top and bottom
- **Eyes:** 5/16 Mirage Eyes

Matt ties large streamers using the least amount of materials to attain the desired profile. A key to success in the musky fly-fishing game is not getting worn out, and this entails being able to fish hard all day and still be ready for a take. "I hear guys talk all the time about how physically demanding it is to cast musky flies," Matt says. "If you have the right rod and line combination and you're not casting a wet sock, it's really not that difficult."

The Yard Sale is an example of this lightweight design, with weight added to the back of the fly. The large plastic rattle provides enough weight to create the desired action without overweighting the fly for casting and fishing purposes. The overall lightweight design of this pattern coupled with the weight in the rear causes the fly to drive from the back, similar to hauling a trailer with too heavy a load. The back (trailer) will want to drive the front (truck), causing the fly to swim side to side, or walk the dog. While it can be fished aggressively, it is most effective with a long strip and pause. The long strip pulls the fly forward, and the time it takes to start the next strip allows the fly to fall to the side. The next strip pulls the pattern in the opposite direction, giving it the side-to-side action that muskies love. The key to properly fishing this pattern is the pause that allows the fly to fall from side to side between strips. ■

JUMPIN' JACK FLASH

- **Rear hook:** 5/0 spinnerbait hook
- **Thread:** 210-denier Danville to match color of fly
- **Tail:** Healthy amount of Holographic Flashabou
- **Rattle:** Large plastic rattle
- **Rear body:** Reverse-tied bucktail with Ice Wing layered over sides and top, with 4 turns of Predator Wrap in between the bucktail to reduce the amount of bucktail while maintaining the fly's profile
- **Connection:** 60-pound Steelon (coated wire)
- **Front hook:** 5/0 spinnerbait hook
- **Front body:** Reverse-tied bucktail with Ice Wing layered over sides and top, with 4 turns of Predator Wrap in between the bucktail
- **Head:** Laser Dub stacked on top and bottom
- **Eyes:** 5/16 Mirage Eyes

Jumpin' Jack Flash is best fished in an erratic motion. This fly also features the light design and weight in the back but is a slightly bulkier pattern than the Yard Sale, so it doesn't have the consistent walk-the-dog action. But it does swim erratically—diving up, down, and to the side. Mixing in longer pauses helps to attain an erratic action. The extra-flashy tail works well on days when something shiny gets a musky's attention. ■

ELI BERANT started off chasing bluegills and stream trout, but now has settled in on the warmwater predator fish in his home state of Michigan. He has a passion for tying and fishing extra-large streamers for trophy fish. Eli began his own commercial fly-tying business in 2009 and leaves the vise whenever he can to test and develop his patterns on local waters.

OPTIMUS SWINE

- **Hook:** 5/0 or 6/0 Mustad 32608 or equivalent spinnerbait hook
- **Thread:** 280-denier UTC to match color of fly or equivalent
- **Rattle:** Jig rattle on a spider collar arm tied off the back of the hook
- **Tail section:** Synthetic material such as Syn-Yak or SF Fiber reversed-tied, 2 saddle feathers down each flank, and Magnum Flashabou
- **Body:** Rainy's Mini-Me medium popper head reverse-tied and secured by Goop; 7 bunches of bucktail (not reverse-tied), 4 on top and 3 on bottom
- **Head:** Senyo's Laser Dub
- **Eyes:** ½-inch 3D eyes secured with Goop

Note: This fly can be scaled down to 5½ inches on a 3/0 or 4/0 spinnerbait hook and a Mini-Me small popper head.

Eli designed this pattern to fall slower through the water column than a fly with an epoxy head. The Laser Dub at the head of the fly and the popper head in the body accomplished this goal; however, the addition of the popper head near the rear of the hook had an unexpected impact on the action of the fly by throwing off its buoyancy and balance. This gives the fly a dramatic walk-the-dog action when retrieved, making it especially enticing to musky. The Optimus Swine has proven successful on lakes and rivers using floating, intermediate, or sinking lines. Eli ties this pattern in a wide range of colors, including natural combinations, black with an accent color, or really bright and obnoxious schemes such as fire tiger, Mardi Gras, green and yellow, bloody sucker, Willen's Villain, bluegill, and perch. ■

B1G FOOSA

- **Rear hook:** 5/0 Mustad 32608 or equivalent spinnerbait hook
- **Thread:** 280-denier UTC to match color of fly
- **Tail:** Synthetic material such as Syn-Yak or SF Fiber reverse-tied
- **Tail collar:** Clump of bucktail on top and bottom, with 2 saddle feathers and Magnum Flashabou down each flank
- **Rattle:** Plastic jig rattle with collar nub clipped off, secured to the top of hook and wrapped with Estaz to match the color scheme of the fly
- **Body:** 5 sections of bucktail, 3 on top and 2 on bottom, with 2 long saddle feathers down each flank
- **Body collar:** Clump of Finn raccoon hair tied on top and bottom of hook. Finish thread head with a UV epoxy.
- **Front hook:** 5/0 Mustad 32606 or equivalent short-shank spinnerbait hook
- **Connecting wire:** 49-strand .024 nylon-coated wire with 2 beads
- **Back body:** Clump of bucktail tied on top and bottom of hook. Tie off the thread and cut, then slide on a reversed Rainy's Mini-Me medium popper head secured with Goop.
- **Front body:** 7 sections of bucktail, 4 on top and 3 on bottom, with Magnum Flashabou and Krystal Flash down each flank, finished off with a clump of Finn raccoon tied on top and bottom
- **Eyes:** ½-inch 3D eyes. Coat thread head with UV epoxy.

The B1G Foosa evolved from one of Eli's older patterns called the Foosa. The B1G is the Foosa tied slightly larger, articulated, and with a popper head added to the front hook. Like the Optimus Swine, the popper head added to the rear of the front hook creates an enticing action in the water that is enhanced during the strip and pause by the free movement of the articulated rear hook. The B1G Foosa is effective in both lakes and rivers and is best fished on a sinking line. Eli has seen this pattern perform well in several color schemes; some of his favorites are Willen's Villain, black-backed perch, black-backed fire tiger, brown and yellow, bloodsucker, and black and red. ■

JOE GOODSPEED is a full-time professional in the fly-fishing industry. He is an ardent and accomplished angler who places a significant importance on fly design and understanding his quarry. This has translated to some impressive success for musky.

MUSKY THRILLER

- **Thread:** White 100-denier Veevus G.S.P.
- **Shank:** 80 mm Fish-Skull Chocklett's Articulated Big Game Shank
- **Under tail:** Enough bucktail to create significant rigidity and buoyancy to keep the back end of the fly hanging horizontal in the water when paused. Use all the colors of bucktail that will be part of the fly's color scheme with the lightest color first and working in layers that get increasingly longer moving toward the darkest color on top.
- **Tail topping:** High-quality strung rooster neck feathers in 5- to 7-inch range. For this pattern the hackle is 8 bright orange feathers topped by 4 cree feathers extending about ½ inch past the bucktail. Align saddle hackles so that the feathers' natural curve faces in toward the bucktail; this orientation has a significant effect on the fly's profile and movement. The feathers will wiggle in the current but won't splay in different directions when the fly is paused.
- **Body:** Stiff bucktail fibers 4-5 inches long to create volume and color. The head of the fly will cover much of the body material. The body is constructed of 6 clumps of spun bucktail. For the pattern shown, the color scheme is yellow, orange, and brown in that order, moving toward the front and repeated on the front half with the longer fibers. Starting just ahead of the materials tied in for the tail, spin the bobbin to twist the G.S.P. thread tight, then set a 4-inch-long clump of bucktail about as thick as a pencil on the top of the shank, with the tips facing toward the rear of the fly. Make 2 loose wraps around the base of the hair and pull tightly and smoothly to flare the hair 360 degrees around the hook. Secure the bucktail and trim the excess. Provide some spacing and repeat. The bucktail should be about ¾ inch to the eye of the shank after this step is complete.
- **Weight:** A keel weight to create neutral buoyancy, requiring a dumbbell eye with enough weight, in addition to the shank and the hook, to offset the buoyant deer hair in the fly. A larger wool head requires more weight to offset the volume of trapped air space created by a sealed wool head. For a wool head with a 1-inch diameter, a 1⁄20-ounce dumbbell achieves proper balance. Attach the dumbbell eye to the bottom of the shank. The weight should be placed about a quarter of the way back from the front of the fly to create a pivot point when the fly is retrieved.
- **Front hackle:** Orange fins on bottom and a topping of cree neck hackle fibers, same as used in tail. For the orange fins, use 2 bright orange schlappen feathers per side. Tie in on the bottom of the fly next to the dumbbell eyes, facing out 45 degrees like pectoral fins. Wait until after the head is completed to trim these to shape. Tie in a clump of 6 cree feathers about 5-6 inches long right on top of the dumbbell eyes.
- **Head:** Spun white wool roughly the size of a golf ball. The head will compact when trimmed and coated. The wool is added in 3 clumps; the first should have the longest fibers, and each clump afterward can be a little smaller. Comb out the wool and trim it into a gentle round taper similar to a Muddler Minnow shape. From this point, the color of the fly head is created with stringy synthetic dubbing such as Lite-Bright tied in and combed back over the wool.
- **Coating:** Use Goop to coat and finish the head; a fresh tube work works best. Apply a thick bead of Goop around the eye of the hook while not disrupting the dubbing placement. Smooth the Goop over the top of the dubbing with a clean finger without carrying it onto the bucktail. Apply a second coat 5 minutes after the first.

ROUND HEAD

MUSKY THRILLER *continued*

The first layer is for shape and the second for the durability to withstand numerous musky attacks.

- **Eyes:** Flat eyes pressed over a dab of Goop for a few moments until they stick in place. Wipe away any excess Goop at the base of the eye. Next, squeeze some fresh Goop on top of each eye and smear the layer of glue to envelop the entire eye, overlapping onto the wool head. This will appear to be a thick bulge over each eye, but let the fly set this way and dry. The glue will shrink and form an ultra-durable clear protective layer that gives the eye a glassy 3D appearance.
- **Hook:** Gamakatsu treble short-shank round-bend hook; #1 for smaller-profile flies, 1/0 for bulkier flies. Flatten barb for better hookups, fish handling, and personal safety. Attach hook to 2 high-quality split rings to improve spacing of hook from fly.

The head is the key aspect of this pattern, as its construction creates significant water displacement. Joe's objective with this design was to create a pattern that carries in the water like the classic Suick wooden plug. A head with a 1½-inch diameter will make a larger vibration pattern in the water, but a 1-inch-head fly will have more erratic action. Joe prefers the larger-head version in stained water where musky rely on vibration to locate prey, and the thinner-head version in clear water where the fish are more sight oriented. This pattern can be tied in a range of colors and has proven effective in everything from natural sucker colors to combinations of black and purple. The dubbing under the coating can be used to create unique color effects such as darker on top and lighter on bottom or highlights of colors to show more of a mottled marking.

This pattern has proven to be extremely effective, as Joe has amassed a list of impressive catches using this fly. It can be cumbersome to cast due to the dumbbell eyes and water being trapped in the wool head under the Goop coating, but Joe has developed an efficient and consistent approach to delivering the fly. With the head of the line extended past the tip, a touch-and-go water haul on the final backcast combined with a haul on the forward cast delivers the fly with sufficient distance and accuracy.

Joe has also developed a flat-head version of this pattern. Instead of the bulbous head, this design features a front section that also uses Goop for the finish but is flattened as it dries. The flat head creates a fully erratic movement in the water, giving the fly the appearance of an injured or stunned baitfish. ■

FLAT HEAD

PAT COHEN is a full-time professional fly tier from upstate New York. Pat's flies are known for their impeccable quality and design.

MANBEARPIG

(8-inch version)

TAIL SECTION:

- **Hook:** 6/0 Partridge Predator X
- **Thread:** 210-denier white Danville Flat Wax Nylon
- **Tail:** Large Cohen's Attractor Tail, with mono loop through butt section to prevent fouling
- **Rattle:** 5 mm glass rattle
- **Body:** Holographic Flashabou, bucktail, 2 sets of splayed schlappen feathers

HEAD SECTION:

- **Shank:** 35 mm Partridge Predator Shank
- **Thread:** 200-denier white Veevus G.S.P. for deer hair head
- **Body:** Bucktail, Holographic Flashabou, 1 set of splayed schlappen feathers, peacock herl
- **Head:** XL Hareline Aluminum Sea Eyes, stacked and trimmed deer belly hair
- **Glue:** Loon Hard Head

This fly finally came to life after going through multiple transformations before the desired action was attained. Pat worked with other musky anglers to design a pattern that would provide an enticing action while rapidly retrieved with a two-handed stripping method. This proved to be quite effective when working the fly over the top of sunken weed beds. Pat took everything he thought important for attracting a predatory response and blended it into one fly. The pattern features a corkscrew twisting tail that he had designed for some of his other commercial patterns. Flash is built around the tail so that when it spins, the flash moves like a spinner blade. The main body is constructed from bucktail and splayed schlappen feathers to maintain a light weight yet project a solid silhouette. There is a rattle and the pattern is articulated, and it is weighted just enough to help keel the fly and bring it down below the surface.

The stacked deer hair head provides for plenty of water displacement and combined with the light, airy tail materials forces the fly to jackknife when retrieved with a sharp single-hand strip. The balance of weight and the floating quality of the deer head make the fly appear to suspend, making the pattern equally effective with a single-hand retrieve. According to Pat there is no wrong way to fish this fly. A sinking tip or intermediate line is recommended. Pat ties this pattern in three sizes: 12, 8, and 5 inches in length. ■

STEVE MAY is a professional fly tier and dedicated angler from Ontario. For more than a decade, Steve has worked on perfecting the ideal musky fly for his local waters.

½ CHICKEN DINNER

REAR SECTION:

- **Hook:** 2/0 Gamakatsu or other treble hook
- **Thread:** 140-denier UTC to match color of fly
- **Wing:** Long schlappen
- **Flash:** Flashabou

CONNECTION:

- **Wire:** Flexible 7-strand wire, forming a loop
- **Weight:** 1/16-ounce brass worm weight
- **Beads:** 8 mm plastic beads

FILLER TUBE:

- **Tube:** 1-inch piece of large plastic tube
- **Thread:** 140-denier UTC to match color of fly
- **Body:** Polar Chenille
- **Wing:** Bucktail
- **Rattle:** Northland jig rattle, slid on back of tube

HEAD:

- **Hook:** Gamakatsu SC15 or other straight-eye hook
- **Thread:** 140-denier UTC to match color of fly
- **Underwing:** Bucktail
- **Wing:** Steve Farrar's Flash Blend, layered
- **Flash:** Flashabou and Angel Hair
- **Eyes:** 3D Epoxy
- **Covering:** Epoxy, Tuffleye, or Clear Cure Goo lightly around eyes

Steve's musky flies have gone through various phases in an attempt to produce the most effective pattern possible. Early patterns were too small or did not provide a lifelike action that produced consistent results. Steve experimented with large rabbit strip patterns that could be tied to a desired length, but they proved difficult to cast all day. Tying with tubes allowed him to get the length of the fly beyond 10 inches using easy-to-cast synthetic materials. A combination of short tubes with two hooks connected by flexible wire resulted in a long pattern that swims well in the water. The tube was placed over the connecting wire to create a surface for tying.

With synthetic materials at the head, the ½ Chicken Dinner sheds water and is easy to cast. The jointed design with flexible wire allows the fly to snake and turn in the water with a hard strip. While it is a fairly narrow pattern, it shows up plenty big in the water to turn the head of a musky. The pattern pictured here is the "wounded banana" color combination. ■

UNCLE BUCK

REAR SECTION:

- **Hook:** 2/0-6/0 straight-eye spinnerbait or stinger hook
- **Thread:** 140-denier UTC to match color of fly
- **Wing:** Bucktail
- **Flash:** Flashabou

CONNECTION:

- **Wire:** Flexible 7-strand wire, forming a loop
- **Weight:** 1/16-ounce brass worm weight
- **Beads:** 8 mm plastic beads

FILLER TUBE:

- **Tube:** 1-inch piece of large plastic tube
- **Thread:** 140-denier UTC to match color of fly
- **Body:** Polar Chenille
- **Wing:** Bucktail
- **Rattle:** Northland jig rattle slid on back of tube

HEAD:

- **Hook:** Gamakatsu SC15 or other straight-eye hook
- **Thread:** 140-denier UTC to match color of fly
- **Underwing:** Bucktail
- **Wing:** Farrar's Flash Blend, layered
- **Flash:** Flashabou and Angel Hair
- **Eyes:** 3D Epoxy
- **Covering:** Epoxy, Tuffleye, or Clear Cure Goo lightly around eyes

The Uncle Buck is a rattle-, weight-, and flash-filled pattern with a tighter wiggle than a feather-tailed version. The pattern builds on the Bob Popovics Bucktail Deceiver design. The pattern pictured here is the "chartreuse attack" color combination. ■

MIKE SMALL is an avid musky angler from northern New York State. His unique fly patterns have resulted in some impressive catches on his home waters.

HAWG FRAWG

- **Hook:** 5/0 to 7/0 Gamakatsu Octopus
- **Thread:** 5- to 8-pound-test Power Pro or other braided fishing line
- **Tail:** Two 4- to 6-inch-long thin Zonker strips
- **Flash:** Flashabou and ⅛-inch Mylar strips
- **Wing:** Cluster of 2-3 different colored schlappen, saddle hackle, or cape feathers tied in on top and sides of hook curving outward; 6-8 strips of ostrich plume tied in on top
- **Throat:** Marabou tied in on top, sides, and belly; white or lighter colors on belly with some red in front of the white. After the marabou is tied in, the thread should be about ½ inch from the hook eye.
- **Rattle:** Pyrex glass
- **Head:** 4 layers of thin closed-cell foam cut to pear-shaped sections 2 inches long by 1 inch wide at top, tapering to a blunt point at bottom. Glue foam pieces together with Crazy Glue with rattle sandwiched in the middle, oriented lengthwise top to bottom. Glue on mirage or other style eyes. Construct the head first, allowing glue to set up. Glue shaft of hook, press and pinch head to hook, and tie foam in at point.
- **Stinger hook (optional):** If adding a stinger, complete this step first. A 3/0 to 4/0 Gamakatsu Octopus is added to the main hook using approximately 9 inches of knotable bite guard wire. Run bite guard along bottom of shaft from bend to bite guard. Thread it through hook eye, then along top of hook shank extending to the rear. Attach bite guard to hook shank by wrapping it tightly with thread and applying Crazy Glue. Attach wire to stinger hook using a nonslip or uni knot, or attach a heavy-duty snap swivel to allow for changing the stinger hook. The stinger can be lightly dressed with flash and feathers similar to main fly, but shorter in length. Deer belly hair or a small piece of foam tied onto the stinger behind hook eye will keep hook riding in the material of main hook.

Mike lets the muskies tell him what pattern is preferred on his waters. He attempts to achieve a fly that catches sunlight; emits vibrations, spits bubbles, splashes, or pops on the surface; causes water turbulence; and either pitches up and down in a jigging motion or side to side in a walk-the-dog action. If he can hit three or more of these in one pattern, the muskies usually take notice.

Most of Mike's patterns include typical big-fly materials such as bucktail, saddle hackle, schlappen, ostrich plume, Flashabou, synthetic hairs, and marabou feathers, but some materials come from craft and hobby stores. Feathers are added, curving out to allow for fly movement during the pause. Red material is added to the front of the fly to represent gills or blood. In the case of the Hawg Frawg, red marabou is added to the underside of the head area.

The Hawg Frawg can be fished on a floating line with a strip and pause that forces the fly to dip on the retrieve and return to the surface on the pause. The pattern can also be fished on a short sinking-tip line or with a couple feet of sinking tip added to the front of a floating line. After allowing the tip to sink and placing the rod tip in the water, the fly digs deeper with a walk-the-dog action and floats back up. Takes typically occur during the pause. ■

SHANE MAYBUSH is a guide and fly tier from Virginia.

DIRK JIGGLER

- **Front hook:** Swim-bait-style hook large enough to hold a musky
- **Shank between hooks:** 40 mm Fish-Skull Chocklett's Articulated Big Game Shank
- **Rear hook:** 3/0 Gamakatsu spinnerbait trailer hook

REAR HOOK SECTION:

- **Tail:** Saddle hackle and Holographic Flashabou
- **Wing:** Bucktail reverse-tied with Holographic Flashabou mixed in and a few wraps of the webby portion of a soft hackle wrapped in at the front of the hook

SHANK SECTION:

- **Wing:** Bucktail propped up by flex cord with Holographic Flashabou mixed in and a few wraps of the webby portion of a soft hackle wrapped in at the front of the shank

FRONT SECTION:

- **Rattle:** Large fly rattle
- **Underwing:** 3 layers of bucktail, the farthest to the rear propped up with flex cord and the other two reverse-tied with Holographic Flashabou mixed into the layers
- **Hackle:** A few short saddle hackles on side and top
- **Overwing:** Puglisi EP Sparkle Brush barred on top with permanent marker
- **Throat:** Red Flashabou
- **Eyes:** Fish-Skull Living Eyes
- **Finish:** Clear Cure Goo for eyes and lightly coated at very front of fly

This pattern was inspired somewhat by Blane Chocklett's T-Bone, using flex cord to create a large profile without the bulk. It can be fished on an intermediate, sinking-tip, or full-sink line. The fly's design is aimed at converting "bottom huggers" into follows and eventually eating the fly.

The keeled swim-bait-style hook combined with the rattle provides weight in the front section of the fly, allowing it to gain depth when fishing deeper and providing for a head-down, dying baitfish look or action in the water. The back hook can be tied in so that it rides in an upward or downward position. The upward position reduces snags when presenting the fly along the bottom, while the downward position provides an up-and-down combination that increases the chance of a hook point finding the softer tissue in the inside of a musky's mouth. ■

CHARLIE DICKSON is an award-winning fly tier from Western New York.

MUSKY TORPEDO

- **Hook:** 4/0 Partridge Attitude Streamer or similar
- **Thread:** 200-denier Veevus G.S.P., color to match color of fly
- **Tail:** Combination of long schlappen, saddle hackles, Holographic Flashabou, and standard Flashabou
- **Collar:** Tips of the deer hair tied in for the body/head
- **Body/head:** Deer hair stacked, spun, and packed tight to create a buoyant fly. The pattern and colors are controlled by how the deer hair is stacked. Deer hair is trimmed to desired size and shape with razorblade.
- **Eyes:** 3D Molded Eyes, 10 mm or similar size
- **Weed guard (optional):** .023- to .025-inch-diameter monofilament

The Musky Torpedo is a versatile pattern to use when the conditions are right for topwater activity. The pattern was designed to imitate a wounded baitfish, with the long tail feathers providing the enticing movement of a potential meal struggling on the surface. It is best fished with an erratic short, forceful stripping motion. This retrieve combined with the torpedo-shaped head/body allows the fly to dart in various directions similar to a jerkbait, creating the illusion of vulnerability that often triggers a musky attack. The size of the head/body also creates some commotion when retrieved. When prospecting open water, a surface fly that creates a disturbance and makes some noise gives you an advantage.

Different colors can be used to represent a range of prey beyond baitfish, including other surface meals such as frogs, mice, or small birds. Adding the weed guard allows this pattern to be fished along the edge of tight, heavy cover, including protruding logs and thick lily pads. Because a weed guard can potentially impact a solid hookup, the version without the guard is preferred in open water. ■

KEVIN FEENSTRA is an experienced, full-time fly-fishing guide in Michigan specializing in steelhead, trout, and warmwater species. He has developed a fascination for musky in his home state.

POPPERAZZI

- **Hook:** 3/0 Gamakatsu trailer hook
- **Thread:** 210-denier Danville to match color of fly
- **Head:** 1 or 2 large copper sequins threaded on the hook toward the eye
- **Tail:** Krystal Flash topped with Holographic Flashabou, Mirage Flashabou, or other flash of your choice. A rabbit strip can also be used but makes the fly heavy after the hide has absorbed water, making it more difficult to cast.
- **Body:** 3 pieces of flat foam stacked on top of hook to extend past hook eye and cinched down behind the eye to make the foam stand up at an angle. The foam forces the sequins to push up against the hook eye, creating a flat surface. The body is completed with Ice Dub cover where the butt of the foam is tied in.
- **Collar (optional):** A collar of bucktail can be added at the rear of the hook to keep the tail materials from tangling.

No matter what the species, Kevin's flies normally contain an ample amount of flash. This pattern is an example of how flash material can add both visual attraction and movement in the water. Kevin's flies also tend to be fairly simple to construct and often use offbeat materials such as sequins from a craft store.

When it comes to surface fishing for musky, Kevin's success relies on flies that push water as opposed to making an audible pop. This pattern tends to push a wave or wake as it is retrieved across the water's surface, a motion representative of some type of exposed prey such as a small duckling swimming on the surface. This fly and approach work best in the low light of morning or evening when the winds are calm and the water is flat. Overcast conditions can extend the period for surface fishing on calm days. ■

NATE CARR is a dedicated and accomplished musky fly angler from Western New York and is one half of the Brookdog Fishing Co. duo.

BIG JENNA

- **Front hook:** 6/0 or 8/0 Partridge Universal Predator X. To connect the hook to shank, tie the 35 mm Fish-Skull shank to the top of front hook, leaving the rear loop on the 35 mm shank hanging off the back of front hook. Make sure to wrap the shank down tightly and apply superglue; wrapping thread right up to the front eye on the shank will ensure it is locked in. Attach the first Big Game Shank to the rear loop on the 35 mm shank for a solid connection.
- **Rear hook:** 5/0 or 6/0 Gamakatsu Octopus. Rear hook can be attached directly to the last shank or a split ring can be used to allow for changing out hooks if one gets dulled or damaged.
- **Thread:** Black or chartreuse 210-denier Danville or 200-denier Gel Spun
- **Shanks:** Fish-Skull Chocklett's Articulated Big Game Shanks; two 28 mm for body and one 35 mm for front hook-to-shank connection
- **Head:** ⅝-inch Cam Sigler Bubble Cone. Wrap a thread bump behind the eye of front hook, then slide the bubble conehead over hook tip and up to eye of hook (you may need to pinch barb down to do this). Apply a couple of drops of superglue to thread bump and then push and twist bubble cone securely onto thread bump. Add Clear Cure Thick to inside of conehead for additional weight and to help lock the head in place. Glue an eye to each side, then coat entire head with Clear Cure Thin and finish with Sally Hansen's or other non-tacky finish.
- **Body:** Black bucktail and ¼-inch black or chartreuse Chocklett's Body Tubing. Bucktail sections on shanks are tied T-Bone style with body tubing used as dams to prop up bucktail. On the front hook, bucktail sections are reverse-tied Bob Popovics style.
- **Hackle:** 4-5 long grizzly schlappen feathers, dyed chartreuse, or grizzly magnum saddle hackle. Note that the schlappen feathers are not tied in at the rear of the fly but rather at the head behind the trimmed bucktail collar. Hackles should be distributed evenly around the fly, top and bottom.
- **Flash:** Flashabou
- **Eyes:** 10 mm Clear Cure Real Eyes

Inspired by Brad Bohen's Buford and Blane Chocklett's T-Bone, this pattern was developed as a small creek/river fly (Little Jenna) and was then adapted for use on bigger water. While casting to deeper-water banks with an intermediate or floating line, patterns like the Buford often don't sink enough on the first couple of strips unless you wait for the intermediate line to sink first. This fly was developed to solve that issue—the aluminum head provides enough weight to sink the fly on those first strips off the bank while also providing a blunt head to push water.

With such great success on smaller waters, Nate scaled up the pattern in size for use on big waters like the Niagara River, where it has proven to be just as effective. Using fast-sinking lines in heavy currents, this fly will sink farther in the water column more rapidly than unweighted bucktail flies. So far this pattern has accounted for muskies in Ontario, New York, Pennsylvania, and Wisconsin, including some of Nate's largest fish.

The fly's action is similar to a Buford or T-Bone, with the side-to-side kick on the strip and pause. But it also has an up-and-down undulating action, as the heavier head dives slightly on each pause and recovers on the subsequent strip. The long hackles on the fly are tied in toward the head, providing "lift" and keeping the feathers separated. This allows the feathers to flutter more freely at the tips. With the addition of a weed

guard, the fly can be banged into structure like rocks and timber. A rattle can be glued into the inside of the bubble conehead for more noise.

My most productive color schemes have been black/chartreuse, hot pink/blue, white/chartreuse, and cream/brown, with the hot pink/blue combo particularly effective for stained water. All around, black/chartreuse has been the best producer in both clear water and stained. ■

JACOB OTT is a full-time guide in White Sulphur Springs, West Virginia, and fishes a handful of his state's bountiful musky waters.

BIG PINK

REAR SECTION:

- **Hook:** 6/0 or 8/0 Gamakatsu SL12S
- **Thread:** 210-denier Danville pink
- **Wing:** Start with a 2 mm pink foam disc cut to approximately 1 inch in diameter. Attach disc to topside of shank approximately ⅓ of the way to the bend; disc should stand up to flare materials. Main wing is constructed with SF Fiber or a similar synthetic. Tie ⅔ of the material on top of shank. Reverse-tie and fold back so that material flares out and folds over the hook.
- **Flash:** Pearl Flashabou—keep all the flash on the topside of the shank, so that it folds back over the SF Fiber in even layers. Alternate SF Fiber and Flashabou tied in in the same manner until close to eye of hook.
- **Hackle:** Long pink grizzly schlappen feather.
- **Overwing:** Long bucktail tied in behind eye of hook. Reverse-tie so that the butt ends cover all the thread wraps from the preceding clump of SF Fiber. Fold back and tie off to complete rear hook dressing.

FRONT SECTION:

- **Shank:** 45-55 mm Waddington shank
- **Thread:** 210-denier Danville pink
- **Wing:** Close shank with tying thread and superglue and attach another foam disc. Attach a clump of SF Fibers evenly around the shank but keep shorter than the rear section. Attach Flashabou to the top of shank. Alternate SF Fiber and Flashabou until you reach halfway mark on shank.
- **Hackle:** Long grizzly schlappen feather in a complementary color to the side of fly
- **Overwing:** Bucktail reverse-tied around shank until ¼ of shank remains uncovered
- **Head:** #15 Flymen Fish-Mask. At ¼ point on shank, create a ball of large pink chenille or dubbing to serve as the glue in substrate for the Fish-Mask. Attach Fish-Mask with glue of choice, then use Clear Cure Goo to secure at front of shank.
- **Eyes:** 15 mm Flymen Fish-Skull Living Eyes, fire color
- **Junction:** Spro 90-pound split ring

Jacob ties this fly in two separate halves and then joins them with a split ring after completion. He finds it easiest and safest to remount the hook in the vise, attach the split ring to the hook eye, and then attach the shank. Jacob uses a base of flash that matches the color of the fly, with pearl and mirage thrown in for good measure.

This pattern evolved from tube fly designs that Jacob originally used for constructing larger flies. However, his earlier patterns were tied with a lot of materials and were difficult to cast, and forming the head with eyes and glues was time-consuming. He also moved to a single hook because of damage to fish with a multiple-hook setup.

This design allows for a change in halves if a hook gets damaged or the head cracks. Using the Fish-Mask saves on gluing time, and the synthetic materials and the reverse-tie method create a lighter fly with the impression of bulk and movement in the water. Jacob mainly fishes this pattern on a fast-sinking line so that it runs 3 to 10 deep, with a long strip and pause to maximize movement. Hot pink is his favorite color for winter fishing in West Virginia. ■

RICK KUSTICH began fly fishing over forty years ago on the lakes and streams of upstate New York. He spends a significant amount of time each year on the water and has developed a special passion for trout, musky, and steelhead fishing in the Great Lakes and Northwest.

SHEEP DOG

- **Tube:** Large clear HMH Poly Tube, 4-5 inches
- **Thread:** 6/0 UNI-Thread black
- **Tail:** 6-8 white schlappen feathers tied in on either side of the tube so that stems splay outward. White cock feathers can be substituted for schlappen for extra length.
- **Underwing:** White Farrar's Flash Blend tied around tube reverse style, then white synthetic yak hair
- **Overwing:** Black Icelandic sheep over white underwing, tied around the tube but not in reverse style
- **Flash:** Gold Holographic Flashabou
- **Head:** Dumbbell eyes to help sink and keel fly, with short lengths of Icelandic sheep tied on top and bottom
- **Hook:** 5/0 Daiichi 2546 or other straight-eye hook

This pattern was my first attempt at tying a bigger fly to fish for Niagara muskies in the late summer and fall. When it was created in the early '90s, it was tied on a dual hook system connected with single-strand stainless steel wire. Eventually I moved to using tubes for their lightness and the ability to place materials to the rear of the fly. The original pattern had a wing constructed entirely of Icelandic sheep, but at some point I added a synthetic underwing with a reverse tie for additional bulk. The synthetic wing also adds sheen and subtle flash. I prefer to position the hook point just behind the end of the wing material so that it doesn't become entangled.

This pattern was designed to imitate a golden shiner—a significant food source for Niagara muskies. It has also been effectively tied all in black, gray and white, and fire tiger. The pattern does not have a lot of bulk and tends to condense in the water, but this has never detracted from its effectiveness. In fact, I have hooked more muskies on this fly than any others. I have moved to using many patterns with shanks, but I still maintain this pattern in my rotation as a good change of pace.

With its fairly sparse design, the pattern is easy to cast. Making effective casts, even late in the day when fatigue is setting in, is a key to success. I will often switch to this pattern after a full day of casting begins taking its toll on my body. Making good presentations with a smaller, easier-to-cast fly is more effective than struggling with a pattern that is difficult to deliver in a repeatable, effective manner.

In warmer water this pattern is most effective when fished with a hard strip and pause. The tube causes the fly to turn to the side at the end of the strip, giving a musky an enticing side view. The tail feathers condense on the retrieve and splay back out on the pause, providing extra movement, and the Icelandic sheep moves and flows in the water even when the fly is nearly at rest. A fish will often pick up the fly on the pause. In colder water the pattern is effective with a slow strip, creeping it along or near the bottom structure. ■

MEGA CLOUSER

- **Hook:** 2/0 or 3/0 Daiichi 2546
- **Thread:** 6/0 UNI-Thread grey
- **Eyes:** Dumbbell eyes tied on top of hook shank so fly rides point up
- **Underwing:** White synthetic wing material such as Steve Farrar's Flash Blend or Kinky Fiber, approximately 5 inches long, tied off in front of and behind dumbbell eyes
- **Flash:** Rainbow Krystal Flash tied in on underside of hook shank for a lateral line
- **Overwing:** Gray synthetic wing material such as Steve Farrar's Flash Blend or Kinky Fiber, approximately 5 inches long

The oversize Clouser Minnow doesn't seem to meet the basic criteria of a musky fly from either a size or bulk standpoint. But early in the season, just after the spawn, I have found that smaller young-of-the-year morsels fit in nicely with a musky's diet as it transitions to its summer waters. Musky also key on smaller bait in the fall as the vegetation dies off, leaving balls of bait exposed to predators.

This simple pattern has provided me with a number of musky over the years in the early season, post-spawn time when fish can be found cruising in shallow flats. These conditions provide sight-fishing opportunity for fish that are eager to rebuild their bodies after the rigors of the spawn. Fished on a floating or intermediate line, the dumbbell eyes allow the fly to sink quickly to the fish's level. Floating or poling over a flat in search of musky provides excitement similar to saltwater flats fishing.

I present the fly well out in front of a cruising musky because it does not look as natural to the fish when presented too closely. While the color illustrated here is effective on the clear water of my home river, the Mega Clouser is also productive in black and brown over white with gold Krystal Flash and in all white with gold Krystal Flash. A bucktail version of the Mega Clouser can also be very effective. ■

PARTY POPPER

- **Hook:** 4/0 or 5/0 Daiichi 2546 or other straight-eye hook
- **Tube:** 3½-inch section of ⅛-inch-diameter clear plastic tube
- **Thread:** 210-denier Danville to match color of fly
- **Hackle:** 6 schlappen feathers
- **Underwing:** Steve Farrar's Flash Blend
- **Flash:** Krystal Flash or Flashabou
- **Overwing:** Bucktail reverse-tied with Icelandic sheep over top
- **Head:** Rainy's Big-Eye Poppin' Head

Because a vulnerable meal can sometimes be found struggling on the water's surface, musky do occasionally feed on top, especially during cloudy or low-light periods with calm conditions. It is therefore a good idea to keep some topwater flies in your box for when the opportunity arises. This pattern is fairly generic and incorporates the same basic materials that I use in most of my subsurface musky patterns. It can be tied in a range of colors. The pattern shown here is designed to look like a large baitfish struggling on the surface. The blunt front end of the popping head pushes water and creates a disturbance on the surface. I fish this pattern with a hard strip to cause a commotion and a long pause.

In addition to baitfish, surface patterns can be tied to represent other topwater meals such as mice, frogs, or even baby ducklings. Of the many manufactured popper heads made of wood or foam available on the market, I prefer those that are large and have a blunt or concave face. Tightly spun deer hair is also a top choice for creating a head. Deer hair allows you to shape the size and contour of the head while creating a color design that blends in with the tail and wing.

While on a trip to Wisconsin, musky guide Dan Boggs showed me a way to convert any fly into a surface popper using a Rainy's Turbo Poppin' Head. These heads have a large hole in the middle that can slide right onto the front of the hook or shank of an existing fly to create a pattern that floats and makes a significant disturbance on the surface. ■

HAM-BONE

- **Hook:** 5/0 or 6/0 Gamakatsu Octopus
- **Thread:** 210-denier Danville to match color of fly
- **Shanks:** Fish-Skull Chocklett's Articulated Big Game Shank; two 28 mm shanks in rear and one 40 mm shank in front
- **Rear section:** 6 long grizzly saddle hackles tied in with 3 on each side of shank. From rear to front, white then tan long bucktail reverse-tied around shank and forced back by wraps of thread; bucktail should be large enough to cover shank. Neatly trim butt ends of bucktail before forcing tips to the rear. Only the front half of the shank is used so that the rear return wire can remain open to allow for changing the hook.
- **Middle section:** From rear to front, first tan, then white, then 2 bunches of tan reverse-tied in the same manner as rear section. Gold Holographic Flashabou tied in sparsely around shank at the front of middle section.
- **Front section:** From rear to front, first white, then 2 bunches of tan, then 2 bunches of dark brown/olive bucktail tied in the same manner as previous two sections. Gold Holographic Flashabou tied in sparsely around shank between the tan and dark brown/olive bucktail. 4 long grizzly hackles tied in on top of the fly with long strands of gold Holographic Flashabou.
- **Head:** #10 Fish-Skull Fish-Mask

This pattern is my adaptation of Blane Chocklett's T-Bone fly. Blane's tying ideas have influenced many of the flies used today to catch musky, and the Ham-Bone has some of the elements found in the typical modern musky pattern. This particular color combination was tied to match the fall, winter, and spring sucker migrations, and the fly pictured here resulted in my personal best musky.

While bucktail flies can be bulky and wind-resistant, keeping the materials fairly sparse will aid in casting. When tying in the bucktail, I use a bunch with the approximate diameter of a pencil. Making one loose wrap followed by tighter wraps allows the material to cover the shank. For a thicker look, a bunch can be added to the top and bottom of the shank with a tight initial wrap. This technique can also be used to create a pattern that has a different color on top and bottom to represent certain baitfish. The Fish-Mask is an easy way to finish this pattern off, allowing me to tie one in a reasonable amount of time for a musky fly. The Fish-Mask also aids in aerodynamics when casting.

This pattern works best with a hard, direct strip and pause that causes the fly to track from side to side. The Ham-Bone has proven to be effective in various color schemes tied to represent baitfish such as golden shiners, perch, and rudd. I have caught musky on black and white, black and purple, fire tiger, and brown/olive and yellow iterations of this pattern. Sometimes I substitute schlappen for the saddle hackle when constructing the tail. Also, Icelandic sheep can be used as the last material added in the front to create a front collar enveloping the fly and providing good movement in the water. ■

CHARLIE GORDON is a full-time guide splitting his time between Virginia and Montana.

GUIDE FLY

- **Shank/hook:** 35 mm Fish-Skull Articulated Shank in front of and behind hook. Rear shank is fastened to hook with a wire loop and a barrel swivel, and bent to 90-degree angle to shorten the length and gain a better grip with the vise without crowding the hair. Hook is NS black 4/0 Gamakatsu heavy cover worm.
- **Thread:** 210-denier Danville to match color of fly
- **Hackle:** 2 shorter saddles in rear and middle section
- **Wing:** 2 colors of bucktail tied in reverse with Big Fly Fiber added to rear section
- **Flash:** Holographic Flashabou added to rear and middle section and a few strands of lateral line flash
- **Head:** Spun deer hair of alternating colors

Charlie's inspiration for this pattern can clearly be found in Blane Chocklett's big fly designs. This pattern is a twist on the T-Bone, designed lighter for clients to handle while still being able to push water. The sparse tie also cuts down on material and the time required for construction. Constructed in true "guide fly" fashion, it takes the sting out of leaving the pattern in a sunken logjam.

The swivel at the junction of the hook and tail section creates additional movement. The short, wide tail vibrates back and forth, its design inspired by Bill Sherer's paddle tail patterns. ■

CONCLUSION

I have been intrigued by musky since I was a young boy, and after nearly five decades, I am no less captivated by this fickle, unpredictable creature that roams waters throughout much of North America. My journey is in no way complete—in many ways it seems like it is merely beginning. As a fly fisher and musky angler, almost every time on the water is like a visit to the classroom. So much has been learned in recent years that I can only hope to keep fly fishing long enough to put it all to good use on waters both near and far.

Musky have forced me to become a better caster, a better tier, and to look at water with an open mind. Musky have forced me to accept defeat while at the same time committing to fish even more intensely the next time on the water. And musky have forced me to pay attention to the little details that can make all the difference.

The opportunity to catch a musky on a fly has never been better. With progressive management by government agencies and the assistance of volunteer clubs, populations are flourishing. Advancements in equipment and flies and the sharing of general musky knowledge on social media have had a springboard effect on the sport. This has spawned a new breed of

It's a sweet feeling to release a fly-caught musky after a successful battle. NICK PIONESSA PHOTO

fly fisher, one that is less concerned about fish numbers and more interested in the hunt and the process. It is an angler who consistently risks bruised egos and an aching body to meet the challenge of landing the most difficult freshwater fish to catch while living in the fly-fishing moment.

Not long ago, fly fishing for musky was considered a fringe element of the sport, but much has changed in a few short years. A fly fisher does not have to be fully dedicated to musky fishing to experience catching one on a fly. The list of knowledgeable professional guides available to put fly fishers on musky water is expanding, but some of the most enjoyment found in the pursuit of musky is figuring it out for yourself. The payoff of a musky encounter on new water that you have researched and planned an attack can provide the sweetest feeling. With the diversity of musky water and the options for watercraft, musky fishing is a sport available to almost all fly fishers.

I suspect that the sport of fly fishing for musky will continue to grow, provided musky stocks remain strong and healthy. Musky anglers must remain diligent to protect their valuable resource. Getting involved in local musky clubs and conservation efforts can go a long way toward improving and protecting key musky waters.

If I were to boil any advice I have on musky fly fishing down to one sentence, it would simply be: Never give up. There will be dry times when you question everything, including why you are doing this in the first place, but success is satisfying on so many levels. One good fish makes the hours of casting worth it. Cherish your successes. And know that the burning desire or even the need to catch the next one is a part of the obsession of musky hunting. What most people may see as insane activity is just another day in the pursuit of musky on the fly.

Musky can certainly be pursued on a more casual level as well. It need not be an all-consuming sport. But for anyone that appreciates the magic of nature, just one close encounter with a sizable musky will probably have you hooked for life.

INDEX

Page numbers in italics indicate photographs.